SNOWCRASH 1997–2003

Introduction by Jane Withers
Edited by Ilkka Suppanen
Written by Gustaf Kjellin

Arvinius+Orfeus

A POSTCARD FROM CYBERIA Introduction by Jane Withers	8
GETTING WIRED	22
SNOWCRASH	42
GOING CORPORATE	76
THE OFFICE	110
SNOWCRASH ON ICE	154
LOOKING FORWARD	182
INDEX The Snowcrash collection	200

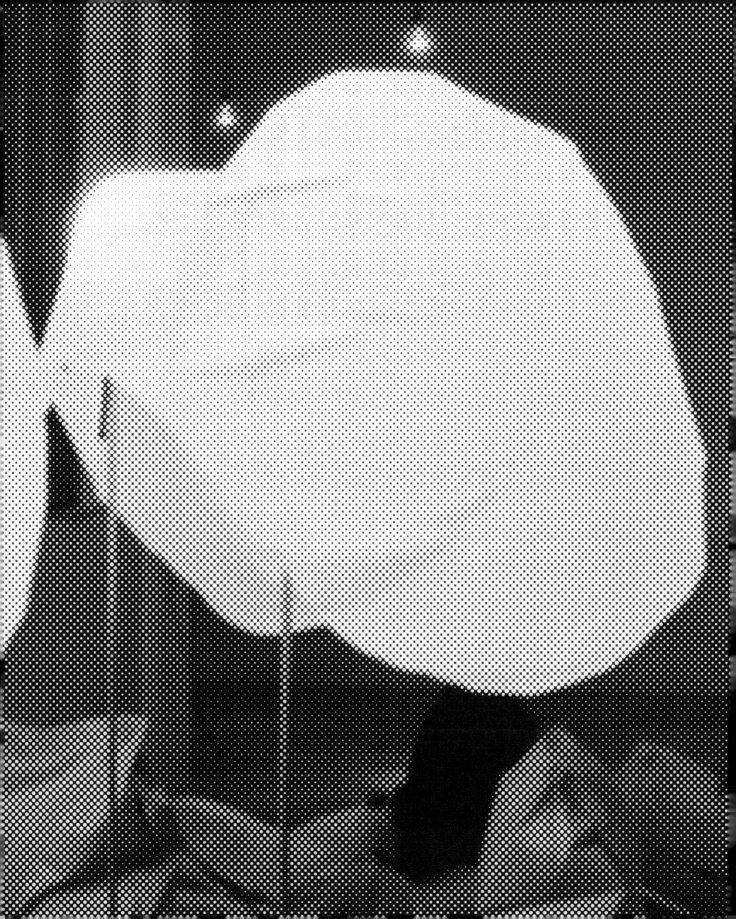

A POSTCARD FROM CYBERIA
Introduction by Jane Withers

1. Iovine V., Julie. 1997. Two Milans: The Retro and the Restless. *The New York Times.* April 17th.

I remember my first encounter with Snowcrash in Milan design week in 1997. In those days the Fuorisalone—the programme of exhibits in spaces around the city—was much smaller than today and news travelled fast of the arrival of a band of Finns with a techie vision. In the Galleria Facsimile in Via Morigi, I wandered into what looked like a campsite for nomadic cybernauts. There was a flotilla of silver *Airbag* cushions and a forest of softly glowing lights that seemed to breathe and gently sigh like exhausted moons. There were curvy snowboard loungers like acid-coloured bananas and an angular 'workstation' that looked like a hybrid between *Easy Rider* and some kind of gynecological equipment, but turned out to be a recliner for computer geeks straddling the World Wide Web (as it was known back then) as if it were a Harley Davidson. The group's name Snowcrash referenced the fuzz of static on a computer screen when software fails, as well as the dystopian sci-fi novel by Neal Stephenson (1992) fusing Sumerian mythology and computer viruses in a 'metaverse' where hackers adopt god-like Avatars and 'Snow Crash' is a drug designed to send its user crazy. And of course, a tongue-in-cheek reference to the designers' Nordic origins and their world class ambition.

That year, Snowcrash was one of several renegade design collectives that attracted attention in Milan and made the reigning stars of the 1990s such as Philippe Starck, Ron Arad and Antonio Citterio suddenly seem, as the *New York Times* noted, like the 'old guard'. In an article titled 'Two Milans: the Retro and the Restless', critic Julie V. Iovine wrote: 'With the same upstart exuberance displayed at this year's Academy Awards, independent furniture designers won the day at the 36th Milan International Furniture Fair, the world's premier annual furniture showcase. And even though the macramé chairs, inflatable room dividers and snowboard divans may never see the light of a mass market furniture store, these conceptually daring, intentionally raw furnishings—the brainchildren of Dutch, English and Finnish designers mostly in their early and mid-20's—came to stand for the way this nomadic generation will be living and designing into the next century'.[1]

At that time Milan's Salone del Mobile was more focused on furniture than it is today. The mainstream hardly seemed to notice the advent of the digital age and Scandinavian design was largely still in thrall to its mid-century masters. In this context, Snowcrash was like an arctic breeze from the land of Nokia, a postcard from a cyber near-future. As well as addressing the design implications of new media, it seemed to promise a new design language born in the pale glow of computer screens and long winters. But it was also a familiar unfamiliar, playing on microgravity; synthetic tech materials; the silvery language of 1960s sci-fi; and the inflatable zeitgeist that was embedded in our imagination of the future via cultural pioneers like Buckminster Fuller's *Cloud Nine* airborne tensile spheres or Ken Adams' set designs for Stanley Kubrick's *2001: A Space Odyssey*. But here in Snowcrash-land, the fantasy was no longer about space and

6-7
The Snowcrash exhibition, 1997

Buckminster Fuller's *Cloud Nine* airborne tensile spheres

intergalactic travel; instead it inhabited the ethereal alchemy of the virtual world, which at that time was ascending to its dot.com zenith.

I came across Snowcrash again a couple of years later when Robert Weil (a phenomenal supporter of the arts and owner of Proventus which also held Artek and Kinnasand) invested in the brand and invited me to collaborate as a long-distance editor, helping to shape what was essentially framed as a utopian design project. Over the next couple of years, I regularly visited their office in Stockholm.

Snowcrash, in common with many avant-garde design movements, emerged in reaction to a rapidly changing cultural and technological context and had the conviction to imagine that things could be different. This was the early years of the dot.com boom and Nokia's success had a catalysing influence on Nordic culture, seeding a dynamic anything-is-possible start-up mentality. With substantial new investment, Snowcrash moved from its organic beginnings in Helsinki to a sizeable new home in a 19th-century factory at Tulegatan 15A in Vasastaden—a central district of Stockholm peppered with vintage modern design stores. While the original Snowcrash collective of Finnish architects and designers Ilkka Terho, Teppo Asikainen, Timo Salli and Ilkka Suppanen remained involved as consultants, they were joined by a support team and several external designers, and given an ambitious if slightly vague remit to grow this maverick tech vision into a design company.

In the sparsely furnished loft, it seemed like everyone had drunk the Kool Aid, and the Panglossian atmosphere of Wired optimism was genuinely seductive. Ideas seemed to emerge from practice rather than theory, flowing endogenously as the designers experimented with new furniture typologies and ways of working, connecting and occupying space that reflected the fast-changing needs and aspirations of their tech peers. Arguably this was as much about imagining new identities for the digital universe as serving the functional needs of cyber workers.

From the outset, several defining Snowcrash characteristics were apparent. Perhaps most obvious was a sense of lightness, transformation and mutability. The *Globlow* light (Vesa Hinkola, Markus Nevalainen and Rane Vaskivuori, 1996) was little more substantial than a white nylon sack on a metal pole, but when the built-in fan was switched on it gently inflated to take on a mesmerising power. *Nomad Chair* (Ilkka Suppanen, 1994) was simply a swathe of grey felt secured on an impossibly slender steel base. It emerged from Suppanen's need for lightweight collapsible furniture when he was a student at the Gerrit Rietveld Academy in Amsterdam, moving from home to home with no permanent abode. *Firebox* (Timo Salli 1999)—a gas flame caught in a glass cube as if a glacier was self-combusting—was a magical take on the elemental, an implausible conjuring act that spoke of sorcery and enchantment. Ice, permafrost, arctic tundra and the poetics of weather were frequent references in Snowcrash design and also featured in the brand imagery. *Cloud* (Monica Förster, 2002) was an inflatable meeting room that looked as if a lone Cumulus had floated indoors—a spectre of 1960s inflatables that took on new currency in the 1990s with the rise of the cloud metaphor for networked infrastructure and virtualised services. *Jack in the Box* (Timo Salli 1997) was a screen that rose on scissor hinges from a semi-transparent box that looked like a crackled glacier.

Technical materials were part of this metaphysical language, borrowed from high performance equipment and sportswear. Suppanen's *Hi-Wave* (1999), a snake of white light hanging in the air, uses a sail fabric, a blend of polymers where the synthetic fibres are laminated rather than woven. The silver textile of the *Airbag* mattress is intended for tents and so extremely durable on the ground. *Globlow*'s shade is made from a lightweight parachute textile. *Soundwave* acoustic panels are moulded from a synthetic felt commonly used in the car industry. Borrowing from more technically advanced industries, the designers were able to develop a distinctive Snowcrash material language that stood apart from the wood, metal, glass and stone typical of furniture and interiors of the period.

If the impact of new technologies was hardly apparent in Milan's design gatherings in the mid-1990s, it was celebrated in the exhibition *Workspheres: Design and Contemporary Work Styles* at MoMA in 2001 in which Snowcrash featured. In *Workspheres*, curator Paola

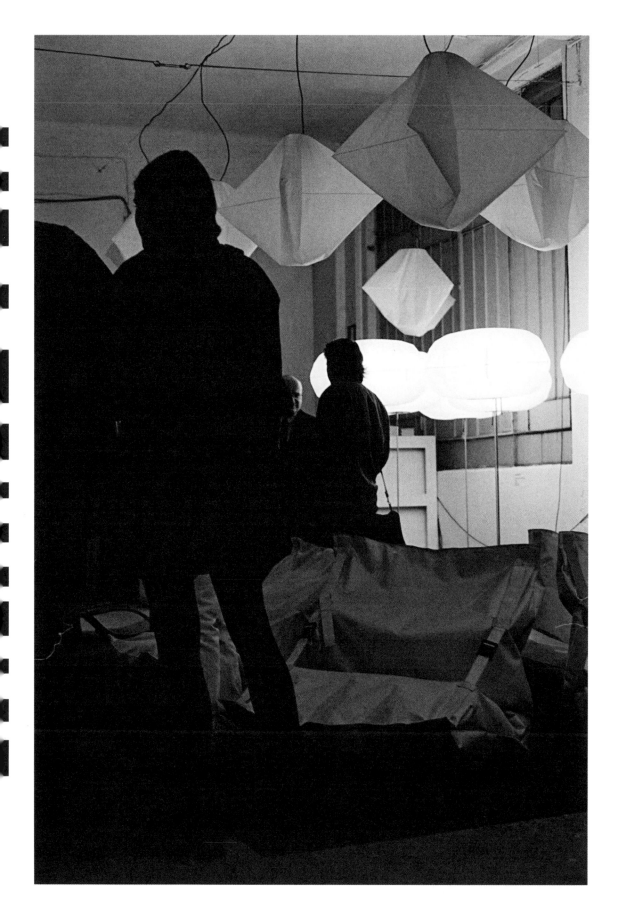

2. Thackara, John. 2001. Designing the Space of Flows. Antonelli, Paola (editor). *Workspheres: Design and Contemporary Work Styles*. New York: Museum of Modern Art / Thames and Hudson, 36.

Antonelli surveyed the changing face of design and technology and explored the impact of new media and the networked economy on work. As mobile technologies, the internet and the cell phone made it possible—in theory at least—to work from anywhere, mythologising around the cyber nomad was powerful. The catalogue cover featured a lone figure seated in an empty parking lot working on her laptop. In the essay 'Designing the Space of Flows', John Thackara observes: 'Our dilemma is this: we have fashioned an urban, networked, complex, and constantly mobile society in which the qualities of space, place and time are given too little attention'.[2]

Not surprisingly, this was fertile ground for youthful disruptors. Snowcrash's emphasis on the horizontal and low level challenged the conventions of the office. The slouchy supine posture of the cyber surfer lounging on an *Airbag*, rocking on *Chip* or straddling the *Netsurfer* like a motorbike suggested a radically different and more playful and collaborative way of being from the upright world of the white-collar workplace with its emphasis on the chair and all that embodies in terms status, hierarchy and power structures.

The *Netsurfer* (Teppo Asikainen, Ilkka Terho 1995) was exhibited at MoMA on a circular plinth in splendid isolation, and it was tempting to read this as a metaphor for the heroic cyber surfer forsaking the physical world for the cyber. Already though, the large rectangular processor looked clunky as bytes and storage had begun to migrate to the cloud and the image of the lone surfer had given way to more sociable visions of cyber connectivity and collaboration. Other Snowcrash designs in *Workspheres* included a wall of gently undulating felt *Soundwave* panels presciently designed to address issues of noise in fluid open-plan meeting and relaxing spaces.

When Snowcrash expanded into larger offices in Hammarby—a former industrial district in the process of transformation, gashed by bulldozers and building sites—the new home designed by fledgling architectural practice Tham & Videgård Hansson was intended not only as a showroom, but also as a site of experimentation and demonstration for their growing interest in less tangible aspects of the work environment such as acoustic and air quality. The entrance had a beautiful wall of *Soundwave* panels.

In the end though, Snowcrash's tenure in Hammarby was short-lived. Despite considerable investment and two CEOs drafted in from international furniture companies, Snowcrash was unable to realise the transition from prototype to production, to convert this youthful flourish of brilliance into viable products for the workplace. Eventually the funding stream of a benevolent benefactor was exhausted and in January 2003 it was announced that the company would, with an aptly cryogenic metaphor, be 'put on ice'.

Looking back two decades, this brief Snowcrash flourish almost seems like a mirage. While a couple of Snowcrash products are still

The Snowcrash exhibition, 1997

manufactured (*Globlow* by David Design and *Cloud* and *Soundwave* by Offecct), many of the new furniture typologies and approaches to creative 'breakout' spaces that the collective pioneered have entered into mainstream workplace design.

But arguably the real Snowcrash legacy is in the vision it both created and reflected of the early cyber age and the dot.com boom. Writing in December 2020, it is ironic that it has taken the disruptive force of a pandemic to normalise the hybrid virtual/physical mode of being that Snowcrash envisaged. But looking in the rear-view mirror, the naïve optimism of the early cyber age seems almost unimaginable. From today's perspective it is hard to recall a time when the internet was not overshadowed by negative impacts on individuals and society, from cognitive development, information overload and social alienation, to the larger spheres of political influence, cyber security and big tech monopolies. But through Snowcrash we can glimpse how it was back then, at the brink of the new millennium, and see what might have been. The collective's most iconic designs made the 'old' world seem static and cumbersome in light of this virtual counterpart and, like Alice going *Through the Looking Glass* to discover what the world is like on the other side of a mirror's reflection, Snowcrash seemed to offer a portal to an altered virtual reality.

Jane Withers, London, December 2020

15-19
The Snowcrash exhibition, 1997

GETTING WIRED

1. This is Finland, *Finland's Weather and Light*, https://finland.fi/life-society/finlands-weather-and-light/ (2019-01-02)
2. *Statsminister Esko Aho talar till Finlands folk* [Prime Minister Esko Aho Speaks to the Finnish People], 1993-01-01, Svenska Yle Arenan, 2011-06-06, https://arenan.yle.fi/1-50103438#autoplay=true
3. *Arbetslösheten 16,9%* [Unemployment 16,9%], Svenska Yle Arenan, 2016-03-10, Fellman Ida, https://svenska.yle.fi/artikel/2008/02/27/arbetslosheten-169
4. Asikainen, Teppo. Helsinki 2018. Interview May 2nd.
5. Nevalainen, Markus. Helsinki 2018. Interview May 2nd.
6. Terho, Ilkka. Helsinki 2018. Interview May 2nd.

20–21
Teppo Asikainen in *Netsurfer* prototype, 1995

In Finland, on the first day of 1993, when the daylight in the south of the country lasts for barely six hours, and the sun won't even bother to rise above the horizon in the north[1], Prime Minister Esko Aho delivers his New Year's speech to the people on *YLE*, Finland's national television platform. His words are uttered with a stern face and with his eyes fixed deep into the camera: 'despite the fact that there are no short cuts to better occupation, we must not give up. I am especially concerned about youth unemployment; if it continues much longer, a whole generation is at risk of being lost in this country'.[2] Before that year came to an end, the official unemployment figures released by the government would say that close to 17% of the Finnish population who were fit to work were unemployed.[3] The collapse of the Soviet Union in 1989 following the fall of the Berlin Wall, had brought down banks in Finland and the Finnish government had dived in to save them—bringing its citizens with them in the plunge and sending the country into a deep recession.

The unemployment that Prime Minister Esko Aho referred to concerned all types of jobs. Aspiring architects enrolling at the Faculty of Architecture at Helsinki University of Technology in the late 1980s were more or less guaranteed a job upon graduation. But then the Finnish bank crisis happened, and people were laid off rather than hired. In 1989, a group of like-minded students in their twenties had found each other during their first year of studying architecture. They formed a loose knit work community and set up a studio in an old cable factory in the central part of Helsinki, formerly used by Nokia, that had been turned into a popular meeting and work space for artists.

'School was very theoretical, we were supposed to get the practical experience from architecture offices during our studies and after we graduated, but the situation being as it was, that was not possible, so we had to find this experience ourselves. We got a space at the cable factory while still studying and started to do our own projects; it became like an extension of the school for us.'[4]

'We could see that architects' offices had already started to lay people off when we enrolled in 1989. Most of our friends who had graduated couldn't find jobs, and the ones who were laid off remained unemployed. So we had to find work ourselves somehow. Maybe half of us in the group didn't even think that graduation during that time was all that important.'[5]

Having had their eyes set on designing buildings, they now had to look for alternative ways of using their creativity to find projects, gain experience and make a living.

'Being 25 years old, I didn't want to accept the fact that there was no future for architects, so if there were no buildings to be designed, then let's design furniture! It felt like the best thing at the time. We had seen what designers like Ron Arad and Marc Newson were doing and it looked so different from 80s design, so that was very appealing.'[6]

Making drawings in the new CAD (computer-aided design)

7. Asikainen, Teppo. Helsinki 2018. Interview May 2nd.
8. Hamngren, Inga; Odhnoff, Jan och Wolfers, Jeroen, 2009, *De Byggde Internet i Sverige* [They Built Internet in Sweden], 2nd edition, ISOC-SE,18-19
9. Hamngren, Inga; Odhnoff, Jan och Wolfers, Jeroen, 2009, *De Byggde Internet i Sverige* [They Built Internet in Sweden], 2nd edition, ISOC-SE, 23
10. Hamngren, Inga; Odhnoff, Jan och Wolfers, Jeroen, 2009, *De Byggde Internet i Sverige* [They Built Internet in Sweden], 2nd edition, ISOC-SE, 38
11. Hamngren, Inga; Odhnoff, Jan och Wolfers, Jeroen, 2009, *De Byggde Internet i Sverige* [They Built Internet in Sweden], 2nd edition, ISOC-SE,40-42
12. Green, Dave. 1995. Demo or Die!. *Wired Magazine*, January 7th, https://www.wired.com (2020-03-03)
13. Steenberg, Eskil; independent researcher and developer. Stockholm 2020, Interview January 30th.

software that came onto the market, the group were able to make advanced objects and designs at a low cost. They worked with strained budgets and instead of buying existing furniture for interior projects, they built their own prototypes and used the latest laser cutting techniques to make custom made furniture in small series. Soon they were working as a fully functioning entity and the assignments kept coming in. So in 1993, despite all the doom and gloom, the group took fate into their own hands and registered the company Valvomo Ltd.

'Valvomo is a Finnish word that loosely translates to a control room or a place where you keep on going. It was a fitting name because we didn't sleep much during those years, we were working hard and hungry for everything new in technology.'[7]

Part of what kept them awake was the emergence of the internet, and just like the snow, this came early to the countries up in the north. Internet can be regarded as a gathering of computer networks, connected with each other through the help of other computers (routers), which allows them to function as one big virtual net that expands through the increase of users. From the beginning, this net was small and used by researchers and teachers to connect with each other at universities in the USA.[8] During the 1980s, universities in the Nordic countries created nets for the same purpose, for research and teaching. These Nordic nets joined together to create one big net that was called NORDUnet,[9] that got wired in to their American counterpart. By doing so, the first parts of an open internet outside of the USA was created and gave countries like Finland and Sweden a head start in digital connectivity in Europe.[10] In the early 1990s Finland and Sweden also gradually deregulated their telecom markets, leading to a quick development of services and applications for using the internet. This happened as an increase of companies and regular folks—not necessarily interested in research—wanted to go online, which also led to a commercialisation of the internet.[11]

Despite the fact that there were no computer developers based in the Nordic countries, an early tech-culture, miles away from Silicon Valley, flourished here. Plenty of days with darkness and bad weather kept young, educated people who could afford to have a hobby, indoors. This gave birth to a generation of skilled bedroom programmers who—for fun—pushed their Amiga, Commodore or Atari home computer to the max to make demos (short for demonstration)—sequences with graphics and music, written with as little code as possible. This generated a 'demo scene' that was concentrated in, but not limited to, the Nordic countries.[12] Programmers on the scene gathered to show off their skills at 'demo parties' such as *Assembly* (1992) in Finland and *Dreamhack* (1994) in Sweden. Then 'LAN parties' (Local Area Network) became a part of it when the computer game *Doom* was released in 1993, which—through connecting computers together—popularised gaming against each other.[13]

'Internet was kind of starting at this time and we were all following

14. Asikainen, Teppo. Helsinki 2018. Interview May 2nd.
15. Terho, Ilkka. Helsinki 2018. Interview May 2nd.
16. Terho, Ilkka. Helsinki 2018. Interview May 2nd.
17. Asikainen, Teppo. Helsinki 2018. Interview May 2nd.
18. Kaplan, Karen, 1995, The Cutting Edge: Computing / Technology / Innovation: Longer Leash: Soon There'll Be No Escaping the Office, *Los Angeles Times*, October 4th, https://www.latimes.com/archives/la-xpm-1995-10-04-fi-53238-story.html (2020-02-04)

it very closely—everything that happened with that and gaming was big for us. When we could afford better computers we connected them in a LAN at our studio so we could play computer games against each other—sessions that would go on all night.'[14]

Everyone at Valvomo's studio knew how it went. You started in an upright position and at the end of a session, you were slouched down in the chair with a sore back. Ilkka Terho and Teppo Asikainen envisioned a furniture with a reclined seat in which the computer would be like the engine.

'I imagined it just like a Harley Davidson, with the computer between your legs—going fast on the information super-highway.'[15]

In early 1995, Teppo Asikainen and Ilkka Terho started to design a piece of furniture in which you could sit in a reclined, comfortable way while using your computer for work, gaming and surfing the World Wide Web. They called it *Netsurfer*. Naturally, *Netsurfer* first came to life as a 3D rendering, with the advantages of its use pedagogically illustrated in a poster-sized collage. As it happened, not long after that Teppo Asikainen and Ilkka Terho got the chance to present their poster to the owners of a showroom situated at the Pacific Design Center in Los Angeles, which sold Finnish design. The showroom owners quickly asked if a real one could be made to be shown in September that year at the trade fair Alternative Office Exposition. Teppo Asikainen and Ilkka Terho said yes and decided—while they were at it—to also present *Netsurfer* at the Finnish furniture fair Habitare in the same month. When building the prototype, they thought of how it could be manufactured on a larger scale and therefore strived to keep the number of expensive mould parts to a minimum. Some of the parts they managed to do themselves, while others could be made with the help of Finnish manufacturers, even though their orders were small. And so September and the day to present their work at the Habitare fair came, and with it, also the very first reactions from the design community: 'A lot of the official establishment design people didn't like it; they basically said they hated it'.[16]

'*Netsurfer* wasn't "against" anything; we didn't try to change Finnish design or anything like that. We didn't even keep track of what was happening on the design scene in general. We just got a lot of our ideas from the things that interested us and for *Netsurfer* we were thinking of an optimal way to use our computers.'[17]

Despite some mixed reactions at the fair, it had seemed that the press liked it, and in any case, next stop was West Hollywood and the Alternative Office Expo at the Pacific Design Center. The theme for this fair was 'Where you sit is where you work' and *Netsurfer* soon caught the attention of journalist Karen Kaplan of the *Los Angeles Times*: 'Speaking of comfort, a pair of 27-years-olds from Finland has designed something called a *Netsurfer*, an alternative to the traditional desk and chair that actually encourages workers to slouch in front of their computers'.[18]

GETTING WIRED

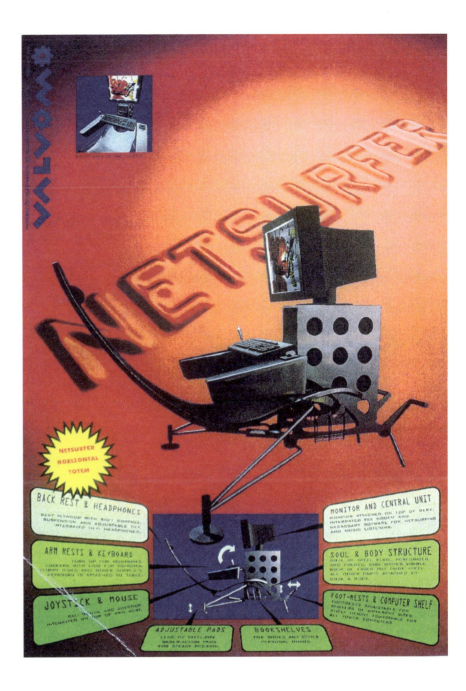

Ilkka Terho testing the seat, and *Netsurfers* being built in a garage, 1995

The poster for *Netsurfer*

19. Asikainen, Teppo. Helsinki 2018. Interview May 2nd.
20. Nevalainen, Markus. Helsinki 2018. Interview May 2nd.
21. Asikainen, Teppo. Helsinki 2018. Interview May 2nd.

1995 had been a good year. Finland had started to crawl out of recession, joined the European Union and won the World Championship in ice hockey for the first time ever, beating its neighbour Sweden four to one. It was also the birth of the *Netsurfer*, and it was obvious to Teppo Asikainen and Ilkka Terho that it had been more in its natural habitat on the American west coast, so close to the home of computer culture, than at the fair in Helsinki.

'We knew of course at the time that there was no real future for this kind of product in Finland, so we had to look outside if we wanted to make it.'[19]

The Habitare fair had given them two new fans however. The chief curator at the Museum of Applied Arts in Helsinki, Kaj Kalin, who had seen a breath of fresh air in *Netsurfer,* and design manager Ahti Antikainen, who not only saw a new expression but also a business opportunity. Not long after the fair, Ahti Antikainen proposed they set up a company to produce it, and so they did: Netsurfer Ltd. They also agreed to continue to try their luck outside of Finland and made plans to exhibit at Salone del Mobile in Milan the following year.

1996 started with a comic-inspired design exhibition at the Museum of Applied Arts, which had caught the attention of Vesa Hinkola, Markus Nevalainen and Rane Vaskivuori at Valvomo. Inspired by the way light was stylised in comics, the three of them wanted to materialise that feeling in a real lamp.

'We tried to create a silhouette with a bag of some sorts. But blowing air inside a bag was nothing new and to gain enough air from the heat produced by a lightbulb would take ages, so we borrowed a fan from one of our computers. We sewed different shapes from a textile used for parachutes, which is lightweight but still strong enough to contain the air, giving the appropriate opacity to diffuse the light source. The lamp really had this extra feature because it took on a new shape every time it deflated, like it was alive.'[20]

The lamp got the name *Globlow* and while it came to life, Teppo Asikainen and Ilkka Terho had detached the large plywood seat from their *Netsurfer* and modified it with a rubber material underneath, so it could be placed on the floor and gently rock. They named their new lounger *Chip,* and presented it in the same exhibition as *Globlow*. *Netsurfer*, *Chip* and *Globlow* were then packed up and sent down to Milan for the fair.

Teppo Asikainen and Ilkka Terho had never been to the fair in Milan, and even though they both easily would have qualified as 'young', the section highlighting young designers at the fair, Salone Sattelite, was another two years away. Instead, they had got a 20 square metre booth in a remote corner of the fair grounds, where they displayed the Netsurfer Ltd collection.

'When we had finished setting up our booth and the fair opened, we quickly realised that we might actually pull this off, as what we were showing was so different from the norm.'[21]

GETTING WIRED

Chip in different colours

Globlow floor version

22. Terho, Ilkka. Helsinki 2018. Interview May 2nd.
23. Salli, Timo. Helsinki 2018. Interview May 2nd.

Word about their booth started to spread; business people came, some press came, and best of all, some orders came: 'It was crazy, we actually got orders from places like South America and Asia. Basically I think it was because they all saw a business opportunity. *Netsurfer* had to do with computers, something which until then had almost all belonged to the geeks. But this was rapidly changing because everybody was getting a PC in their home, and so we strongly felt that furniture paired with technology was a hot topic'.[22]

With their confidence boosted, they went around Milan to see the exhibitions, talking and comparing what they were seeing, and they started to feel that things were not as dark as it seemed in Finland at the time. During one of their evenings of doing the rounds at the showrooms, they met two friends from Helsinki, Timo Salli and Ilkka Suppanen.

Timo Salli was a licensed welder with a passion for art and construction, who through friends had gradually become interested in furniture design. At the time of the Salone del Mobile in 1996, Timo Salli was working on his MA thesis at the Helsinki University of Art and Design, and he quite unknowingly shared the same attitude towards design as the Valvomo crew. One of the objects in his thesis, which revolved around objects made for the living room, was a cabinet/table with a TV that could be retracted into the table via a remote control, named *Jack in the Box*.

'My point of origin was that the TV had replaced the open fire. Our eyes are automatically drawn to the moving flame, which with time became the moving image. And the idea was that you had to put away the TV in a very concrete manner to actually understand that you are not looking at it anymore, that you are not addicted. It was an act, a low-tech choice in a digital world. People who saw it said "it is so interesting when it comes up", but I was thinking the other way around—it is so interesting when it goes down—because then you get the freedom and the peace.'[23]

It was at the Helsinki University of Art and Design that Timo Salli had gotten to know and become friends with designer Ilkka Suppanen. Ilkka Suppanen had begun studying architecture in the late 1980s and later moved on to study design. Since 1995 he had been working out of his own studio and had already attracted a great deal of attention with his designs, in particular an easy chair that at the time was called *Seat 1 and 2*. While attending the Gerrit Rietveld Academie in Amsterdam in 1992, he had experienced the need for light and flexible furniture, due to far too many temporary and crowded living arrangements. So he designed an easy chair for himself, made out of the absolute bare minimum of material, that could easily be dismantled and reassembled. He brought the easy chair with him (as hand luggage) when moving back to Finland and refined the design in the coming years. The final version had a seat made of thick felt that was supported by a structure of spring steel. It was the very embodiment

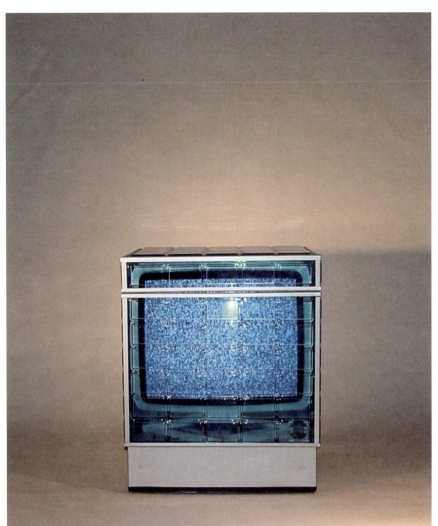

24. Salli, Timo. Helsinki 2018. Interview May 2nd.
25. Suppanen, Ilkka: Helsinki 2018. Interview May 2nd.
26. Asikainen, Teppo. Helsinki 2018. Interview May 2nd.
27. Terho, Ilkka. Helsinki 2018. Interview May 2nd.

of the increasingly widespread urban nomadic lifestyle, and therefore he named it *Nomad*.

Timo Salli and Ilkka Suppanen had travelled down to Milan to check out the exhibitions and the international competition of their profession. They knew most Nordic companies were exhibiting at the fair in Cologne, but had heard that the fair in Milan was a bit more of an artistic scene that also made room for one-off pieces.

'I think many studying design at our age were a bit fed up with Finnish design history; our teachers just kept doing these plywood chairs with wooden legs. Perhaps it wasn't so conscious but I think Ilkka, just like me, felt that we wanted to explore other expressions and materials. That is why it was so healthy for us to go to Milan in 1996, because we were working on our projects and objects and then we experienced this open-minded scene and felt that there actually could be a place for our kind of designs.'[24]

And then one day at a café (or perhaps it was nighttime in a bar), Teppo Asikainen, Ilkka Terho, Timo Salli and Ilkka Suppanen sat around a table in the midst of the design capital of the world.

'We sat there and talked and said to each other that, actually, what we are doing in Helsinki is not so bad compared to what is being shown here.'[25]

'We started talking about design in general and I think we all said that we could do better than some of the companies showing there. It was my first time in Milan and maybe I had expected more from it. So we had this feeling that we should try and come back there and just break the bank.'[26]

'Teppo and I had got a really good feeling from the visitors to our booth at the fair and we felt exhilarated. So we all said something similar, agreeing to come back here in a big way next year!'[27]

And for the following two nights, they met up and started talking about the exhibition that they were going to do together, and what they would call it.

NOMAD CHAIR - Ilkka Suppanen, 1994

CHIP - Teppo Asikainen, Ilkka Terho, 1996

STASH

SNOWCRASH

1. Suppanen, Ilkka. Helsinki 2018. Interview May 2nd.
2. Asikainen, Teppo. Helsinki 2018. Interview May 2nd.
3. Suppanen, Ilkka. Helsinki 2018. Interview May 2nd.

Back home in Helsinki, some 2000 kilometres away from the generous showroom receptions where they had been elbow to elbow with the design world, Teppo Asikainen and Ilkka Terho immediately rolled up their sleeves and started to build *Netsurfers* to meet the orders from the fair. The four friends also started to plan their return to Milan. The basic idea was to show pieces that each of them had been working on individually, all presented together in a joint exhibition. Based on what they had experienced in Milan, they all felt that what they were working on was different; they were immersed in everything that the digital world brought them and shared an interest in new materials. In their own respective ways they had responded to and interpreted growing needs in a rapidly changing society, and looking at each other's works, they could easily see them side by side. Now everybody started to make alterations, finish up old prototypes and realise new ideas to make a collection that would—as they had so clearly agreed upon in Milan—break the bank.

'The future, which to us was digital, seemed so bright and full of possibilities and I think that our designs reflected that in different ways. The road to our exhibition in Milan was a typical story of being young and unafraid and starting something without realising how much work it will be.'[1]

'When we came back from Milan we took it very seriously, had meetings regularly, and also involved the rest of our friends in Valvomo. We spent a lot of time talking about how the exhibition would feel with objects, images, graphics and sound. And the name was important for us, because it would frame everything.'[2]

In an alternative dystopian present, envisioned by author Neal Stephenson, people are spending most of their time in the 'Metaverse', an online social plattform experienced through goggles hooked to computers. Navigating the streets of this Metaverse is Hiro, a free-lance hacker and former employee of a high-tech Silicon Valley firm. Moving in and out of the 'real' and 'digital' world, Hiro finds himself rampaging through California, trying to stop the outbreak of a virus posing as a drug called 'Snow Crash'. When exposed to the virus—a digital scroll with a binary code hidden in a black and white bitmap—in the Metaverse, one's computer and brain are completely scrambled.

Neal Stephenson's sci-fi novel *Snow Crash*, published in 1992, was given to Ilkka Suppanen by a friend who urged him to read it. Ilkka Suppanen liked it, the title most of all, and suggested it to the rest of the group, who all agreed it was a fitting name for the exhibition.

'I think we all realised that no one would ever remember our Finnish names, so it was better to just use one name. We were inspired by the title of the novel; it worked for us because we felt that what we were creating was somewhere in between two worlds—the tangible and real and the digital and unknown. The word "snow" also played with people's image of the Nordic countries, and the word "crash" was a little bit like us, crashing the party in Milan.'[3]

40–41
The Snowcrash silver shirt, front pocket

4. Nevalainen, Markus. Helsinki 2018. Interview May 2nd.
5. Terho, Ilkka. Helsinki 2018. Interview May 2nd.
6. 1994, Sähkö Recordings Interview, Alien Underground –Techno Theory for Juvenile Delinquents Version 0.0. Issue November/December (UK zine premiere issue). https://datacide-magazine.com/sahko-recordings-interview-1994/#more-1685 (2019-08-13)
7. White, Michelle. 2014. Sähkö 20 Years Anniversary Special Interview with Mika Vainio & Tommi Grönlund. *Mosaic Theory.* February. https://cargocollective.com/mosaictheory/Sahko-20-Years-Anniversary-Special-Interview-with-Mika-Vainio-Tommi (2019-08-13)
8. Realsoft Graphics. *Some History of Realsoft.* https://www.realsoft.com/history/ (2019-09-03)

Having seen product launches at the many galleries and showrooms in Milan, they knew they needed to be in the right place to make an impact. Ilkka Suppanen asked for help from a friend who was teaching at the Helsinki University of Art and Design, Matthias Dietz, a design manager from Germany, and explained what the group was up to. Matthias Dietz' immediate response was that if something like this were to be done, they would need somebody that could help them on the ground in Milan. So he connected them with Studio Viterbo Relazioni Stampa, a well established PR firm with decades of experience of working with major furniture companies such as Cassina, Driade and Vitra. The owner of the company, Mariangela Viterbo, suggested that they rent Galleria Facsimile, an alternative art gallery in central Milan where names such as Ron Arad had previously exhibited. Back in Helsinki, this sounded good, and they began to work out their budget.

'We started to apply for different grants in order to get financial help, but we just didn't get any. The reactions we got were to the contrary, that perhaps we shouldn't do this exhibition at all. We weren't playing by the rules basically—it was different from the way Finland usually presented design abroad, so some organisations got upset.'[4]

'When we started to talk about our plan, people would say things like "Whose permission do you have to go and make this exhibition?" and "You are architects, not designers—what right do you have to do furniture?" But we didn't care—of course we didn't need anybody's permission.'[5]

Feeling that they had no official backup from the Finnish design community, they went rogue, emptying their bank accounts and taking loans to pay for the project themselves.

Everything for the exhibition had to be done in the best possible way and to the best of their ability to create a complete experience. They started to engage friends within the creative scene in Helsinki—like fellow architect Tommi Grönlund who was also running a record label called Sähkö Recordings. Sähkö (electricity) Recordings, was an underground record label founded in 1993 by Tommi Grönlund and the musician Mika Vainio (1963–2017), and it had become known among a small but devoted crowd for its pure minimalistic electronic sound.[6] The Snowcrash group asked Tommi Grönlund for some ambient music to be played in the exhibition room, and he suggested that Mika Vainio compose it. Mika Vainio had been active as a DJ in the Acid House scene, throwing illegal warehouse parties in the early 1990s,[7] and had recently found success as part of the group Pan Sonic with their album *Kulma* (1996). Under the alias Ø, Mika Vainio delivered on cue a 34:16 minute sound that would connect the objects and enhance the ambience in the room—the Snowcrash Soundtrack. One of the popular 3D programs at that time was *Real3D.* This was a piece of software created by two Finnish brothers in 1989 that had become an international commercial success due to its high rendering quality.[8]

9. Polster, Bernd (editor). 1999. *Design Directory Scandinavia*. Pavilion, 282
10. Lindén, Carl-Gustav. 2015. *Nokia och Finland: rapport från de galna åren* [Nokia and Finland: a report from the crazy years]. Schildts & Söderströms, 157

Everybody at Valvomo used it, and one of its members, Timo Vierros, took it upon himself to create a short animated loop with snow flakes that could be projected onto one of the white painted gallery walls like a digital fresco.

Everyone working on the exhibition was well aware of how contemporary Finnish design was perceived abroad. It was the classics in glass and wood that people knew about, maybe with the exception of Finland's enfant terrible, Stefan Lindfors, who had become the international face of young Finnish design when his lamp *Scaraggo* was picked up by Ingo Maurer GMBH in 1988. As far as the group was concerned, Finland had not excelled in any notable way in the international design community. One exception, however, was Nokia, which everyone agreed could be credited for lifting Finland out of recession. In the mid 1990s, Nokia mobile phones were connecting people at an increasingly higher tempo, making Spanish guitarist Francisco Tárregas Gran Val's interlude reverberate around the globe. And with no less than 32 new telephone models being developed in 1997,[9] Nokia was well on its way to becoming a world leader on the mobile phone market. Founded in 1865 as a pulp mill in the town of Nokia in southern Finland, Nokia's success had become a symbol for the renewal of Finland—putting it on the world map as the nation that had embraced new technology and turned it into a natural part of their lives.[10] 'Finlande number one' read the headline in an article in French newspaper *Le Monde* in March 1996, which hailed Finland as a the

The *Snowcrash Soundtrack* CD

Still from *Digital Fresco* animation

11. Kahn, Annie. 1996. Finlande number one. *Le Monde*. June 23rd.
12. Melgin, Elina; Ph.D, Managing director, ProCom – Finnish Association of Professionals. 2020. Telephone interview March 17th.
13. *Snowcrash*, 1997. Press release. March.

model country for technology with the most internet users per capita in the world.[11] This was also what the Snowcrash group wanted to take advantage of and communicate to the international design community in Milan. To help them come out in the right way and with the right words, they hired Elina Melgin, head of the communications unit at the University of Art and Design Helsinki.

'I think it was quite unusual at the time, at least in Finland, for designers to work so consciously with PR, especially if you were as young as they were. I functioned as a mirror for their thoughts and I began to formulate the sentences around their concept. And if you want to make a crash you have to wait for the right moment, so our collaboration and most of what they did were kept a secret until it was time to come out. They were also very careful in which press to approach, instead of the mass media they wanted the "right" media to cover them.'[12]

The headline of the press release read *Snowcrash / New Finnish Design*, carrying the tag line 'From the land of snow and cellular phones come designs for a virtual living room of the future', and in the following text they made it clear what they were all about:

'Outdated ideas about Finnish design still seem to flourish in Europe, so Snowcrash will certainly provide a surprise or two for designers and the general public alike. No bent plywood here, but instead visionary articles for an age of networks …Snowcrash is an imaginary trip to a future moment when the computer screen is suddenly filled with static like a snowstorm. With the virtual connection severed, the tangible world becomes real once again…' They also used the subtitle *A Cyborg's Living Room*, to further frame the concept: '…designers Ilkka Terho, Teppo Asikainen, Ilkka Suppanen and Timo Salli have witnessed how the big companies haven't recently been investing in experimental product development. Yet there seems to be a huge need for new creative ideas and innovative visions, also in Milan …the common denominator of the four designers is a shared vision of the relationship between technology and mankind. Counterbalanced by a high-tech rationality, art and design have sought their way to the heart of deep and vital human experiences.'[13]

This had set the bar, and nearly a thousand invitations had been mailed out to journalists, designers and producers in the field in which they now wanted to prove themselves.

A good friend of the group, the photographer Tuomas Marttila, offered to take photos of the objects for free in his studio and the slides were then sent to be duplicated for the press releases. In addition to this, the PR agency in Milan advised them to also arrange one official image photo and the group decided to take the advice even though it would nearly wipe them out financially. The Argentinian photographer Mario Pignata Monti (1951–2018) who had taken portrait pictures of all the great designers and famous new buildings at the time, was hired for

SNOWCRASH

The photo taken for the press by
Mario Pignata Monti

14. Nevalainen, Markus. Helsinki 2018. Interview May 2nd.
15. Suppanen, Ilkka. Helsinki 2018. Interview May 2nd.
16. Asikainen, Teppo. Helsinki 2018. Interview May 2nd.
17. Viterbo, Mariangela. 2020. Email February 25th.

the job. When the super photographer arrived at Helsinki-Vantaa International Airport he had the flu, and with a big scarf wrapped around his neck he finished the crucial photo shoot in an afternoon and then left Finland.

'I don't know what he was thinking about us youngsters, but I remember that he was smoking in the studio while walking around and making final adjustments to the still life he had made with our objects. Before beginning the shoot, he passed the *Globlow* lamp and saw a small thread sticking out from the seam, and he gently took the cigarette from his lips and burned it …no photoshop needed.'[14]

When April finally came, it was showtime. The group had been giving all they had for a full year. A van was loaded with their gear, 14 different designs in total, and it headed south.

'Kaj Kalin had been giving us feedback on our designs along the way and also kind of coached us before our show in Milan. He said things like "when talking to journalists, look scruffy and tired. Don't wash your hair and explain that you have just arrived from a business trip to China or something"—everything to look the part [laughs].'[15]

Galleria Facsimile at Via Morigi 8 in the Carrobbio area of Milan, was owned by the charismatic Horazio Goni, who mostly promoted young artists out of the traditional art system, and the gallery had become one of the top places to show during the fair. The building has a courtyard surrounded by a wisteria covered facade and the gallery is situated in what used to be an old printshop at one end of it.

The design week in Milan in 1997 had not yet grown into zones; instead there were some 300 independent events scattered around the city in beautiful locations. When the group from Helsinki arrived they immediately got to work. But the ancient electric system in the old house on Via Morigi 8 was overwhelmed by the amount of power a cyborg's living room needed, and so when the furniture and equipment were plugged in, the lights went out.

'Timo Salli had to re-wire the whole gallery and build it so we could drag the electricity from the basement upstairs [laughs].'[16]

The exhibition was set up on time and to put the dot over the i, the group all put on specially made silver shirts. They had brought several cases of Vodka with them from Finland, but when someone kindly remarked that drinking it straight would be frowned upon, a deal was quickly struck with the neighbouring restaurant for their house wine to be served instead, narrowly avoiding an outright rager. On the 9th of April, the opening night, the place filled up fast.

'In my opinion it was very well received. Everybody was there, and the international press came in large numbers. Achille Castiglioni came to visit twice, first alone, and being absolutely enthusiastic about the show he came back the next day, bringing Alberto Alessi with him.'[17]

'That opening night was just a dream come true, I remember seeing black cars continuously stopping outside the gallery. I mean, if you look at our background, we were young nobodies, coming from

18. Salli, Timo. Helsinki 2018. Interview May 2nd.
19. Bogholt, Ragne. 2018. Telephone interview May 8th.

Finland where the future for designers looked bleak to say the least. It was crazy because it never normally happens right …that you create an exhibition and then it becomes like that. And then of course the last part is even more crazy because then Ragne Bogholt visited us.'[18]

Ragne Bogholt was a design manager and the CEO of the Swedish furniture company Lammhults. He had been with the company for 25 years, and through progressive product development and new ideas to establish on international markets, he had turned Lammhults into an export success story. Lammhults had been a frequent exhibitor at the Salone del Mobile, but this was the last year that Ragne Bogholt would join them since he recently had left the company to work for Proventus Design. And at the end of the design week, he visited the Snowcrash exhibition.

'I was interested in general in what was happening in the design industry and I heard of the Snowcrash exhibition while I was in Milan. So I was curious and went there to have a look. I thought that what they were showing was a very different way of looking at furniture; it struck me as so new and fresh.'[19]

Ragne Bogholt made sure that he talked with everyone in a silver shirt, and before he left he said to one of them that he would call them.

The Snowcrash silver shirt

The entrance to the courtyard at
Via Morigi 8

51-55
Setting up the exhibition at
Galleria Facsimile

SNOWCRASH

LOGOTYPE

'This design was truly a team collaboration, and I think that if you have a perfect name, then that is nearly everything when making a logo. The whole narrative is the combination of the two words, so we made the logo as simple as possible; it does not even try to be a logo in a sense. I decided to use Franklin Gothic because it was, and still is, one of my favourite fonts. It is straight but possesses a certain kind of positive attitude. If you consider Helvetica, it feels kind of German; Franklin is somewhat warmer even though it is just a simple grotesque. So we put "snow" in regular and then "crash" in italics, and it brought out what the word is about. We used the colours Ice Blue, White and Black and also made a pattern with dots that was part of the logo. To make a pattern like that at the time was pretty advanced stuff, but these days of course it only takes a second.'
-Mikko Männistö

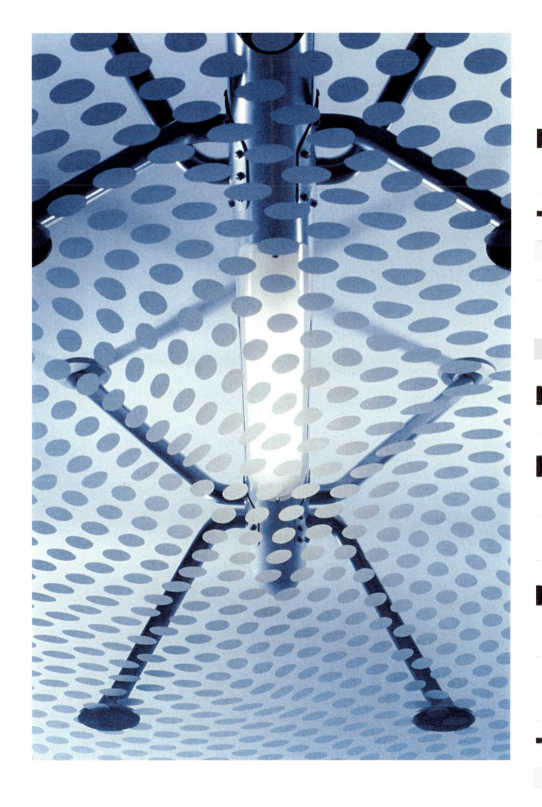

TOMAHAWK, 1997

This was an illuminated glass table comprising: a rocket-shaped body of laser-cut steel; in-built light with dimmer; and laminated glass with titanium oxide blown graphics. Designed and made for the Snowcrash exhibition in Milan in 1997, it served as a table for the DJ.

PLUSMINUS - Jan Tromp, Rane Vaskivuori, 1997

ZIKZAK - Timo Salli, 1997

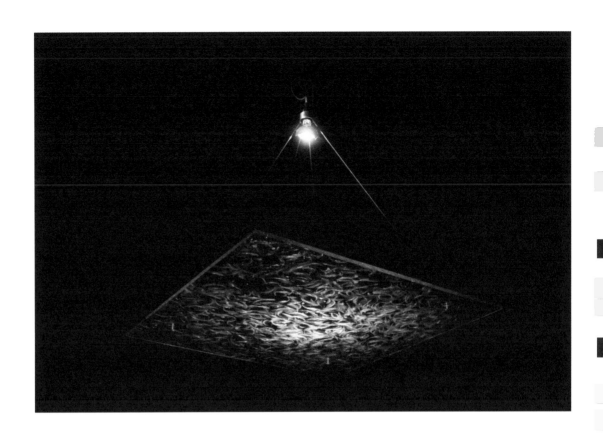

FROZEN FEATHER - Ilkka Suppanen, 1997

FROZEN FEATHER, 1997

'I was visiting a glass factory that also made safety glass, and it was an industrial process where they used resin between the glass sheets instead of a film. I had the chance to try it out and recognised that there was a possibility to mix in thin particles with the resin. Feathers are beautiful in themselves, but you never have the chance to use them, so this was an opportunity to put something fragile in a durable form.' -Ilkka Suppanen

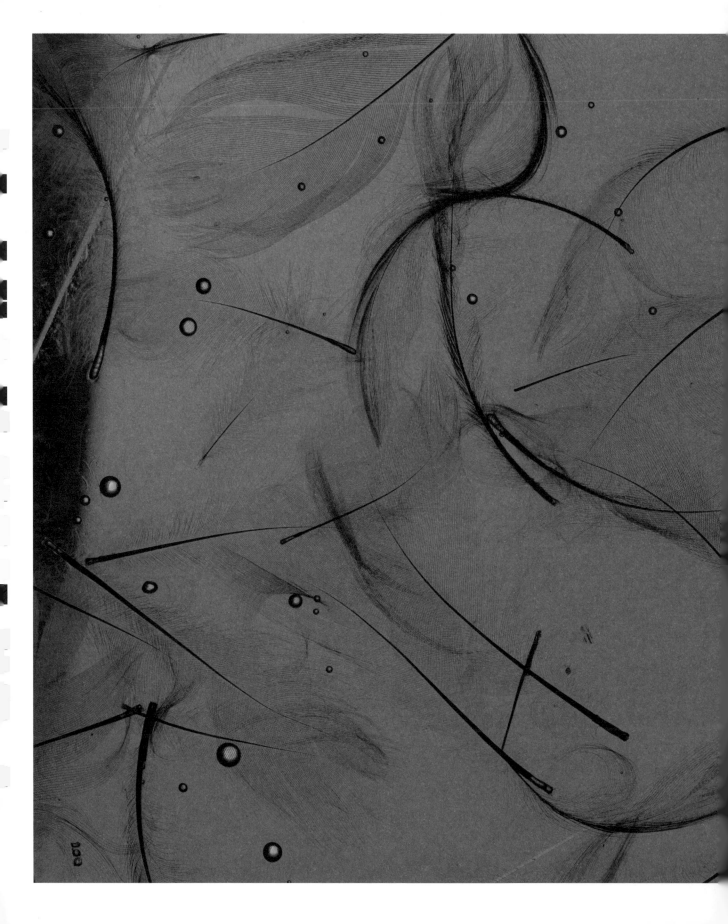

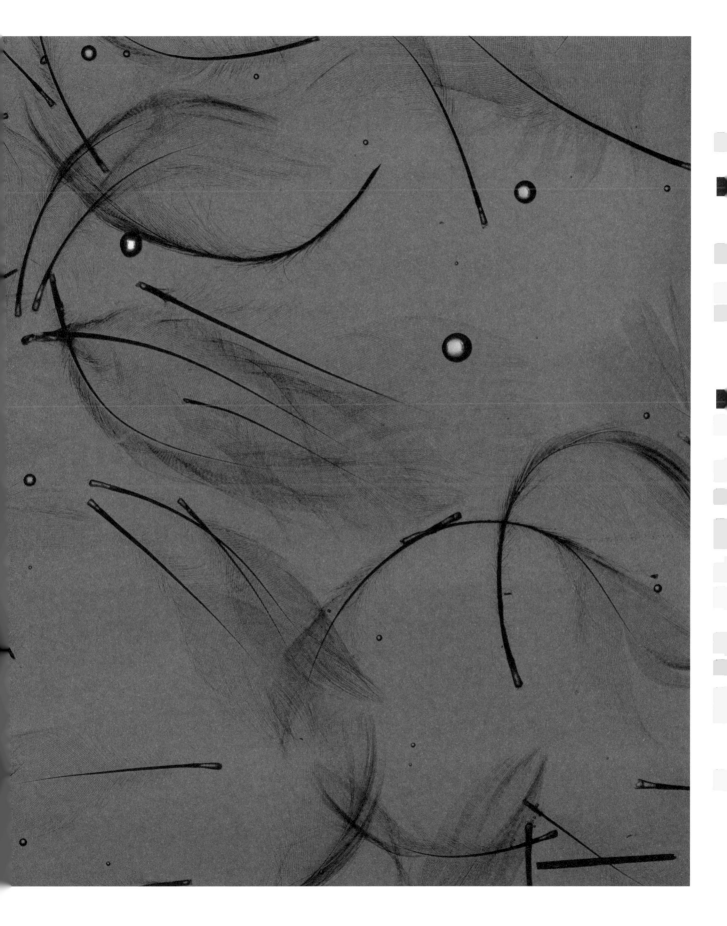

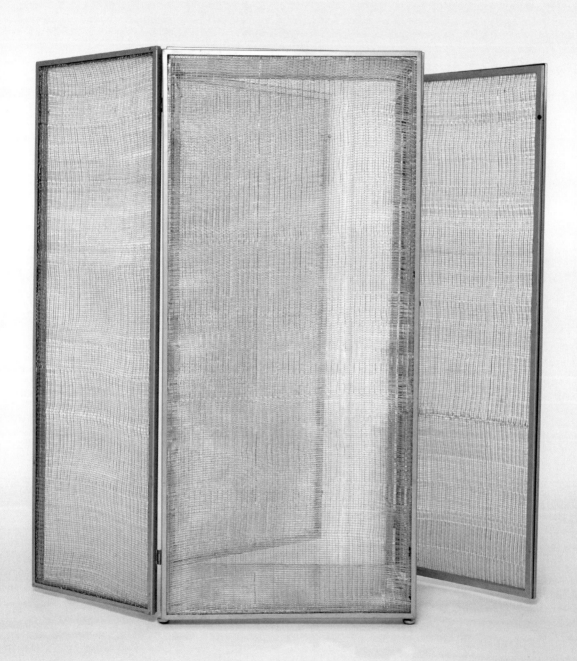

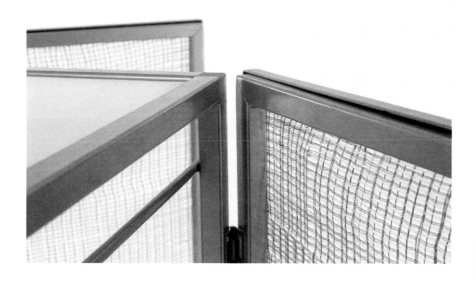

AV RACK, 1997

'We were thinking a lot about how the home would change and adapt to new technology. It was clear that we would own and use more technical products, and I felt we needed newer and nicer furniture to store it in. I imagined a generic version of the traditional audio-visual rack, like a piece of mini architecture with a semitransparent tactile surface, so the visual connection with the indication lamps on the devices was maintained. I was studying technical textiles at university and got to work with fishing lines. I chose two nuances which were then handwoven together with a steel thread in a loom. It was quite labour intensive, but the result was a textile that I could attach to a steel frame to make the cabinet.' -Ilkka Suppanen

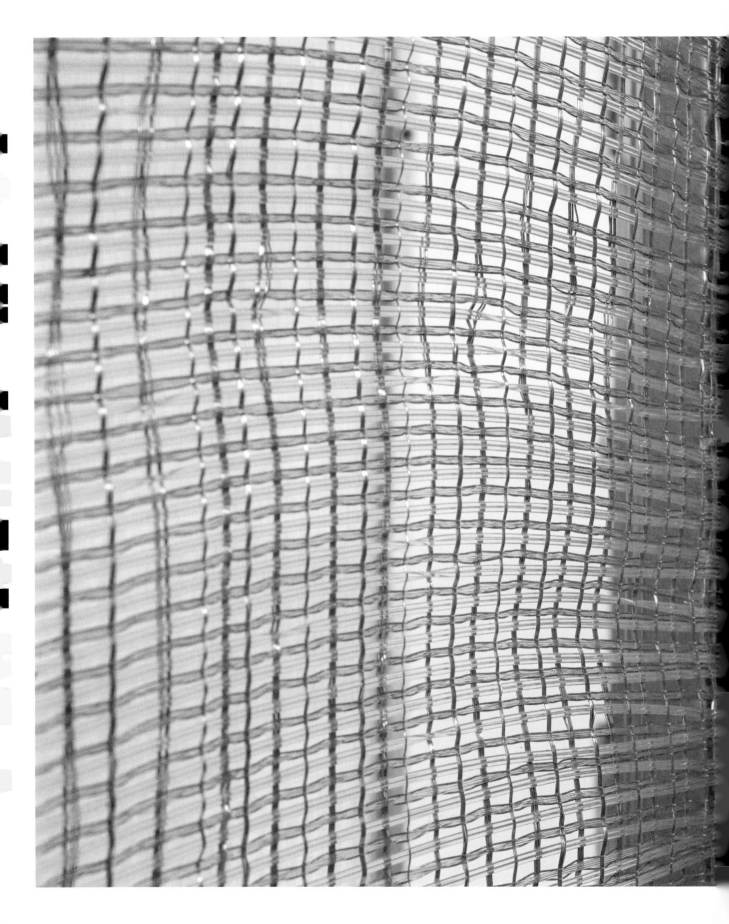

AIRBAG - Pasi Kolhonen, Ilkka Suppanen, 1996

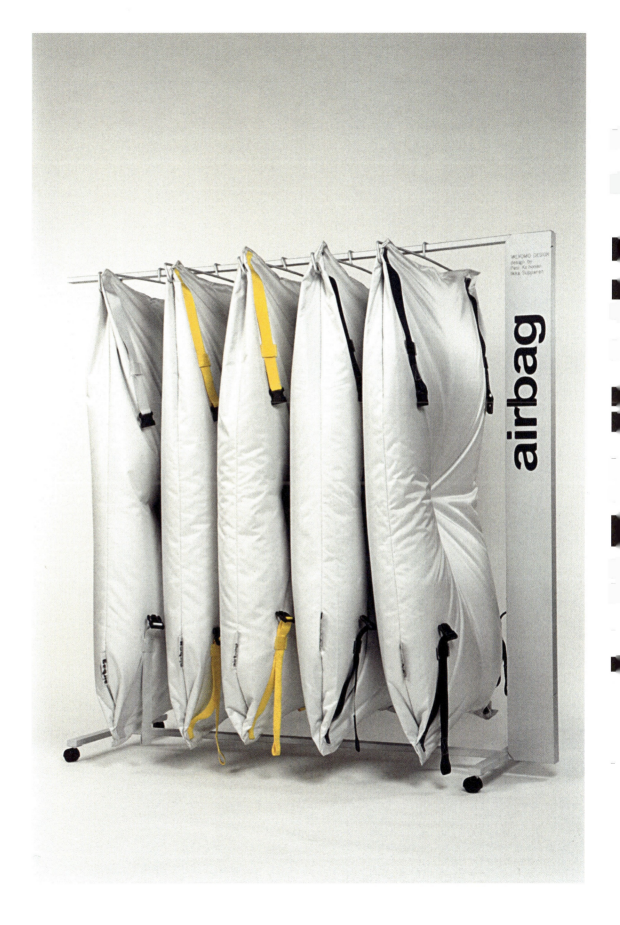

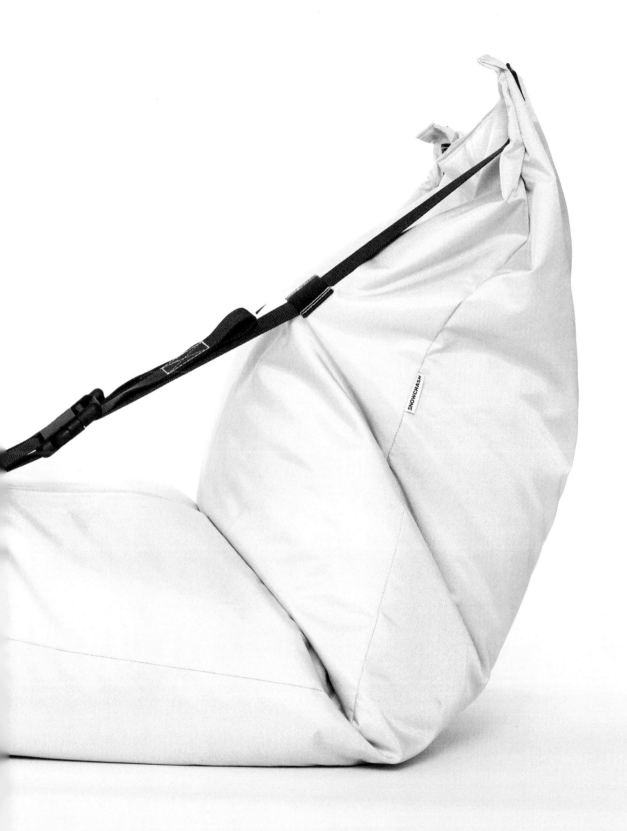

GOING CORPORATE

1. Asikainen, Teppo. Helsinki 2018. Interview May 2nd.
2. Salli, Timo. Helsinki 2018. Interview May 2nd.
3. Terho, Ilkka. Helsinki 2018. Interview May 2nd.
4. Iovine V., Julie. 1997. Two Milans: The Retro and the Restless. *The New York Times.* April 17th.
5. Bakker, Gijs and Ramakers, Renny (editors). 1998. *Droog Design: Spirit of the Nineties*, 010 Publishers, 117
6. Fiorentini, Cristina. 1997. Snowcrash, Modello Finlandia. *DDN.* June issue
7. Sciama, Sabrina. 1997. *Domus.* July/August issue, 795.
8. *Interni.* 1997. July/August issue.

74-75
Flying Carpet sofa, 1997

Back in Helsinki the light on the fax machine in Valvomo's studio flashed red. It was out of paper because it was all on the floor in one big scroll filled with requests, orders, and proposals. The exhibition had been a success beyond what any of them could have imagined.

'We didn't know where this exhibition would take us, we just wanted to open the doors and windows to the world and see what would happen.'[1]

'In Finland there was this mentality that if you succeeded at home then you could try and make it abroad, but we realised we had to do it the other way around. We did, and it worked.'[2]

'Many designers from the older generation liked us and what we had done. They said it was strange that we were working as a group, but that the spirit reminded them of their youth. And if you consider Aalto and Eames attitude towards new techniques and materials, that was really how we also worked, and it seemed people saw that.'[3]

The group could later look through press clippings of their designs being featured with and compared to some of the designers they considered to be an inspiration in the first place. The design week in Milan in 1997 and the 36th edition of the fair had presented the best from the world of design. Recurring names were Antonio Citterio, Ron Arad and Philippe Starck, who were categorised in one article in *The New York Times* as 'the old guard'.[4] Some journalists interpreted the fair by connecting the dots between new furniture made in plastics. There were a lot of them, and the one who stole the spotlight was Tom Dixon with his newly formed production company Eurolounge, and the rotation moulded stool/light, *Jack*. No article forgot to mention Marcel Wanders' macramé wonder, the *Knotted Chair,* shown at Spazio Solferino as part of the exhibition *Dry Tech II*. This was the result of a project that Droog Design had set up in collaboration with the Aviation and Space Laboratory of Delft University of Technology, the aim being to combine low tech aesthetics with high tech materials.[5] But the big news this year were 'the Finns', which was probably something new to put in a headline for many of the magazines that covered the fair and design week. Journalists were also quick to draw parallels between Droog Design and Snowcrash, which this year clearly had represented a juicier tech:

'The products these four young Finns presented at the Facsimile Gallery remind us of the creativity and innovation in the first projects presented by the Droog Design Group.'[6]

'Snowcrash takes us back to Droog Design's first presentation… These refreshing, stormy alternatives are like acid snow on the calm commercial world of the official fair.'[7]

The press was of course not ignorant of the famous Finnish design history, and made a point of this comparison: 'The designs of the Snowcrash collection can be credited with spreading a "revolutionary" image of Finnish design in Europe. The young designers have made a clean, courageous break with the curved wood…'[8]

9. Büttner, Ulrich. 1997. *Moeble interior design md.* June issue
10. Cappellini, Giulio. 2020. Email April 25th.
11. Terho, Ilkka. Helsinki 2018. Interview May 2nd.

The one who perhaps best put it into words, and in the process also unknowingly yet accurately predicted what would happen next, was the chief editor of the German magazine *Moeble interior design md*, Ulrich Büttner:

'Suddenly one's professional curiosity is still alive after 9pm… one ends up in a showroom that registers not the merest hint of studied posing, anticipated success or noble laid-back attitudes …ideas obviously spawned by clear heads, nothing flashy-trashy, but products disarmingly unconventional …every one of them representative of a young, mobile generation of designers and consumers comfortably at home with technology …To me, it's from the approach of designers such as these that decisive impulses will emanate in the future, seeing that they're probing into the needs of society to evolve ideas at a time when the market is content to make do with variations on traded themes. This now, is where manufacturers with a penchant for innovation ought to look out for new opportunities.'[9]

Just as the group had hoped for, besides publicity they also got people to believe in their designs. Giulio Cappellini was one of the many visitors to the exhibition, and being known for having a penchant for innovation, he immediately sprang in to action.

'The presentation of Snowcrash particularly struck me for the innovation of the products on display, both for their image and for the use of materials: light, poetic furniture able to give a new image to interiors. Two products in particular attracted my attention and entered the Cappellini catalogue: the *Flying Carpet* sofa by Ilkka Suppanen and the *Tramp* easy chair by Timo Salli. The first is a product that completely revolutionises the concept of upholstery: made out of a thin layer of wool felt, it rests on a metal structure to create a seat of excellent comfort in contrast to the massive sofas with many paddings. An eco-friendly product that anticipated the times. The second product is light, transparent and completely empty inside: a lesson on how comfort can be created even with few elements. *Flying Carpet* and *Tramp* therefore represented an important moment in the evolution of contemporary design.'[10]

The news of their success had reached Finland, and the group were featured in the biggest newspaper *Helsingin Sanomat*. They were invited to appear on a news show on national television, but the Finnish design producers never called.

'The Finnish furniture industry in general was not so interested in us and it was quite understandable; times were hard financially, and if it perhaps was an old family company that did ok, then why risk things with our adventurous designs?'[11]

A few month after the fair in Milan, the group got 'the' call from Ragne Bogholt, who had not forgotten about the Snowcrash exhibition and wondered if Proventus Design could purchase it.

Proventus (meaning harvest in Latin) is an international investment company founded in Stockholm in 1969 by Robert Weil—a

Details of *Flying Carpet* and *Tramp*

TRAMP - Timo Salli, 1996

FLYING CARPET - Ilkka Suppanen, 1997

12. Proventus. *The Story*. http://www.proventus.se/the-story/ (2019-10-12)
13. Salli, Timo. Helsinki 2018. Interview May 2nd.
14. Terho, Ilkka. Helsinki 2018. Interview May 2nd.
15. Asikainen, Teppo. Helsinki 2018. Interview May 2nd.

man of finance who was driven by an unwavering love for the arts, and who firmly believed in the benefits of merging it with industry. Proventus had a long history of engaging with, and working in, the creative industry. In 1982 they had acquired Upsala Ekeby AB, a conglomerate including Rörstrand ceramics, Kosta Boda crystal glass and GAB Gense cutlery—companies with deep roots in the Swedish handicraft tradition—and turned them around financially. In 1987, Proventus ventured in to the arts scene when establishing Magasin III in Stockholm, founded by David Neuman and Robert Weil—a new and experimental institution that allowed for artists and audiences to engage in unexpected ways. While Magasin III began its journey to becoming one of the most renowned destinations for contemporary art in Europe, Proventus took ownership of the computer and software company Datatronic/Victor Technologies in 1988, which later could be credited for championing innovations such as the removable hard disc drive. In 1992 Robert Weil was approached to help the Finnish company Artek—known for maintaining the legacy of Aino and Alvar Aalto—from going under financially by becoming its majority stakeholder. Artek's 57 year old recipe for arts and technology was something that Proventus not only was familiar with, but also deeply cherished. The following year Proventus acquired Kinnasand, a nearly two centuries old Swedish fabric company, and in 1997 Kinnasand and Artek, now fully owned by Proventus, were organised under Proventus Design.[12] The purpose of Proventus Design was to serve as a mothership for these two companies, to make them grow, cross-fertilise, and in the same spirit as the Aaltos, sow new seeds to design for an age that was now partly being constructed in ones and zeros.

Ragne Bogholt called from the office of Proventus Design in Växjö, situated in the south of Sweden in an area which due to its long history of furniture producers is known as 'möbelriket' (the kingdom of furniture).

'We were actually all together in my studio when Ragne called and proposed to buy what we had shown as a brand. I quickly blurted out a ridiculous amount of money and Ragne replied something like "thank you, we are not interested" and then that conversation was over. We all got nervous so I called back and we later of course came to an agreement.'[13]

'I think we discussed it quite a lot. I personally think that we wouldn't have had enough money and time to become a producer ourselves, so in the end we thought why not give it a try, because why hold this back if we would not use it. We didn't think of what we had done as a brand at all, it was just an exhibition.'[14]

'It was of course quite an exceptional thing that someone would come and take an exhibition and build a company around it. It was better than we could have ever imagined, and we saw quite clearly how a company like Proventus could give this whole thing a push and make things happen fast.'[15]

In September, the movie *The End of Violence* by German director Wim Wenders premiered in cinemas, and in it you can see one of the leading characters, played by actor Bill Pullman, comfortably parked in a *Netsurfer*. It was now a fact—the design by Teppo Asikainen and Ilkka Terho had been firmly cemented in popular culture, an event that placed them in the same exclusive club as their country man Eero Aarnio, whose *Ball Chair* (1963) had also appeared in numerous Hollywood productions. Pieces from the Snowcrash exhibition were continuously exhibited in group shows in different countries, while the conversation with Proventus Design continued and a contract was slowly drafted. As if this year could not end on a higher note, Timo Salli received a letter with an invitation to represent Snowcrash at the annual independence party held at the president's palace—the biggest and most lavish social event of the year.

Even before a contract was signed with Proventus Design, Ragne Bogholt asked the group to make new design proposals for Artek. In 1998, when Alvar Aalto would have turned 100 years old, Artek presented an updated collection at the Salone del Mobile in Milan, of which the stackable chair *Droppe* by Ilkka Terho and *Kromosom* by Jan Tromp from Valvomo were a part.

'Besides asking them to design for Artek, my idea was also that Snowcrash, which represented something new and young, could serve

The End of Violence (1997) Bill Pullman

16. Bogholt, Ragne. 2018. Telephone interview May 8th.
17. Salli, Timo. Helsinki 2018. Interview May 2nd.
18. Bogholt, Ragne. 2018. Telephone interview May 8th.
19. *Snowcrash*. 1998. Proventus Design AB. Press release. October.
20. Bogholt, Ragne. 2018. Telephone interview May 8th.

as an experimental branch to Artek. Some of the furniture from the Snowcrash exhibition could also go to Artek and some could stay in Snowcrash.'[16]

'I thought that it was a good idea to bring in a new generation of designers to Artek, and that it really would not harm the old Aalto collection, but it seemed that there was an opposition within Artek.'[17]

No pieces from Snowcrash entered the collection of Artek and the new designs that were proposed and shown were soon discontinued.

'Artek is a fantastic company that I very much admire. But the deep roots made it hard to bring in new designs. Artek had its own board which decided on the collection, I was of course entitled to come with suggestions, but it didn't really work out. At Artek they simply wanted to hold on to their legacy.'[18]

By October 1998, the deal with the designers behind Snowcrash was finalised and the time had come to officially announce that Snowcrash had been established as a company and joined Artek and Kinnasand within Proventus Design. The headline of the press release read *Proventus Design Establishes Company for Young Experimental Design* and the main message was spelled out in one sentence: 'There will be no limits with regard to what products will be developed, instead it will be a broad selection of products within the interior decoration sector'.[19]

'Snowcrash didn't have the heavy legacy that Artek had; it could start from scratch and be and do whatever it wanted to. Snowcrash was an innovation company where we wanted to let the designers have a great deal of freedom and the possibilities to develop their ideas. I was convinced that the design industry needed this because a lot of companies thought they were doing it—but they weren't.'[20]

The premiere of Proventus Design would take place at the Stockholm Furniture Fair in February 1999. Proventus Design had booked a central location at the fair in a section called Area Modern. The stand was divided between Artek, Kinnasand and Snowcrash, which presented pieces from the exhibition in 1997 as well as a string of new objects. Ten large banners with the text '1+1+1 = 1. Kinnasand Artek & Snowcrash river gränser (tear down borders)' marked the stand. There was some anticipation in the air—within the design community, the Snowcrash exhibition in 1997 had almost become the concert that everybody said they had been too. But the setting and format of the furniture fair in Stockholm was worlds apart from the alternative gallery space where Snowcrash had shown in Milan. This was a regular trade fair, and not a particularly international one at that, where the main draw was the blonde wooden furniture that in the 1990s had become the emblematic image of contemporary Scandinavian design. Here was furniture which aesthetically stood with more than one leg in a modernistic past, made by a generation of predominantly young Swedish producers and designers who had successfully attracted the attention of the international press. Basically, this was the last place to

21. Tarschys, Rebecka. 1999. Framtiden är som en flyglounge [The future is like an airport lounge]. *Dagens Nyheter.* February 11th, 4.
22. Hedqvist, Hedvig. 1999. Gammal stil mot nya tider [Old style for new times]. *Svenska Dagbladet.* February 14th, 18.
23. Zetterström, Jelena. 1999. Form allt viktigare konkurrensmedel [Form, and increasingly important means of competition]. *Dagens Industri.* February 13th, 21.

look for the future, but nonetheless, even though Snowcrash did not fit the bill they were mentioned in the major local newspapers.

'The most futuristic environment at 1999 years furniture fair otherwise comes from Finland via the group Snowcrash...'[21]

'In the middle of the modern area, there is a grand investment, Artek, Kinnasand and Snowcrash, all of them nowadays under the umbrella of Proventus. Artek has long struggled with renewal, but has now searched deep in its drawers and found drawings of Aalto for the sanatorium in Pemar. Maybe once discarded because they reminded too much of Marcel Breuers designs. But here and now, they look surprisingly fresh and are hardly matched by the new launches in 98 and 99. The young Finnish team Snowcrash, which created uproar in Milan in 1997, saves the situation with new light fittings. Snowcrash continues its course and shows us how to furnish with light, poetically and joyfully.'[22]

'The new contender Snowcrash, which is a part of Proventus Design, stands for this fair's most daring, playful and unpredictable design...'[23]

A combined showroom for Artek, Kinnasand and Snowcrash at Tullhus 3 in Stockholm, 2001

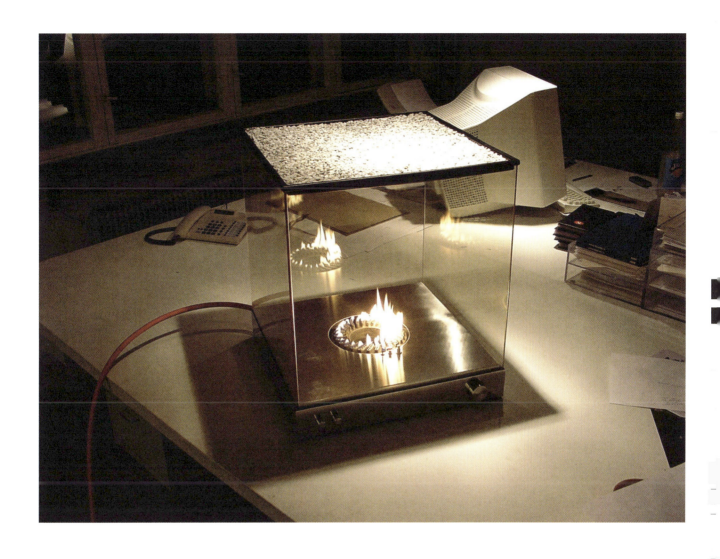

DRESS CHAIR - Rane Vaskivuori, Timo Vierros, 1997

FLY CHAIR, 1999

'The mesh on the chair was industrial screen textile (used in paper making processes), and the upper part of the frame was hardened steel wire.'
-Teppo Asikainen

KROMOSOM CHAIR - Jan Tromp, 1998

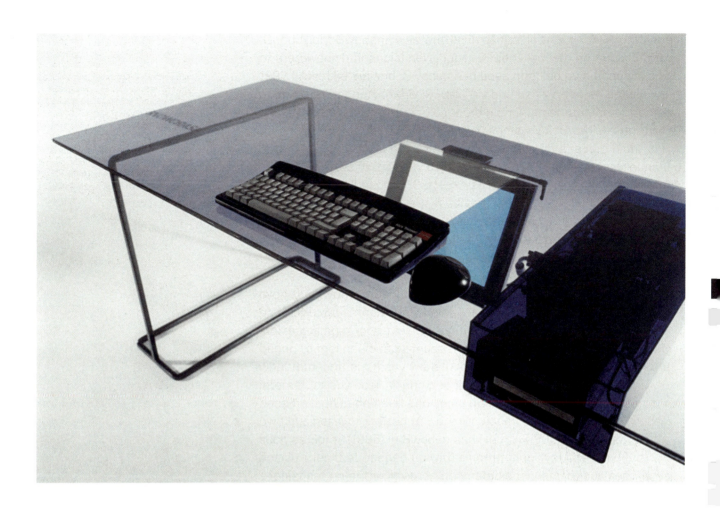

LAMPLAMP, 1999

'The name is kind of a joke because this is a play with two light sources, the natural and electric. The light shield consists of a curved 4mm thick window glass which is basically the same as the ones used in the rear mirrors on big trucks. But I applied only a 60% silver coating on the back side, so it becomes semitransparent, allowing daylight to fall on the wall behind it while also reflecting into the room. When daylight is gone, you can switch it on. The electric light source is a clear halogen tube that measures eight centimetres, a common component in old fashioned industrial lamps used on construction sites. It emits a very nice yellowish light when it is dimmed, like a sunset. The piece casts two geometrical shadows on the wall; it also casts doubt on the viewer watching it, because it becomes unclear what constitutes the lamp and the mirror.' -Timo Salli

TIMOTIMO LAMP, 1998

'This was not so much about the actual product, but more about how far I could take the idea of two- and three-dimensional form in the typology of lamps. It consists of a fluorescent lightbulb encased in a plastic bag that is clear on one side, with UV protection so it does not go yellow with time, and semitransparent on the other side. It is held up by a steel rod frame and the edges are then glued together with a clear gel tape. So this is a flat piece, but then you can customise it yourself by bending the steel frame in different shapes, so it could hang on the wall, lie down or stand up like a sculpture.'
-Timo Salli

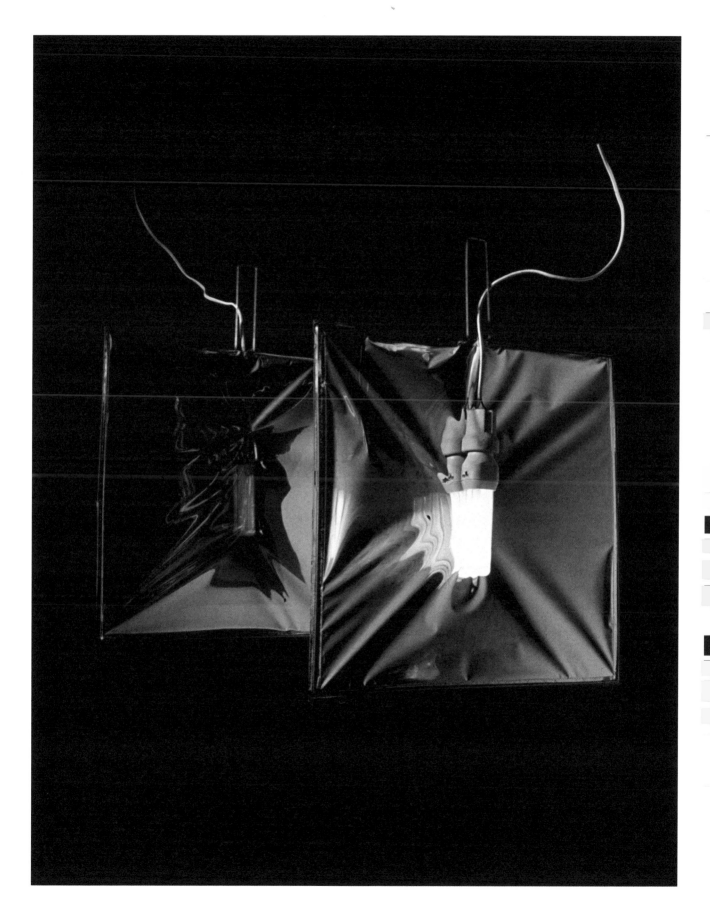

LESS IS MORE – Simo Muir, 1998

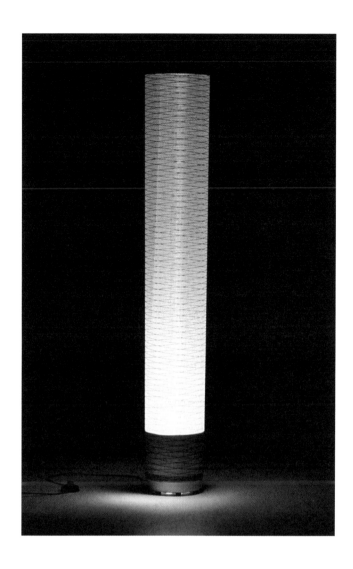

ROLL LIGHT - Ilkka Suppanen, 1998

GAME SHELF - Ilkka Suppanen, 1999

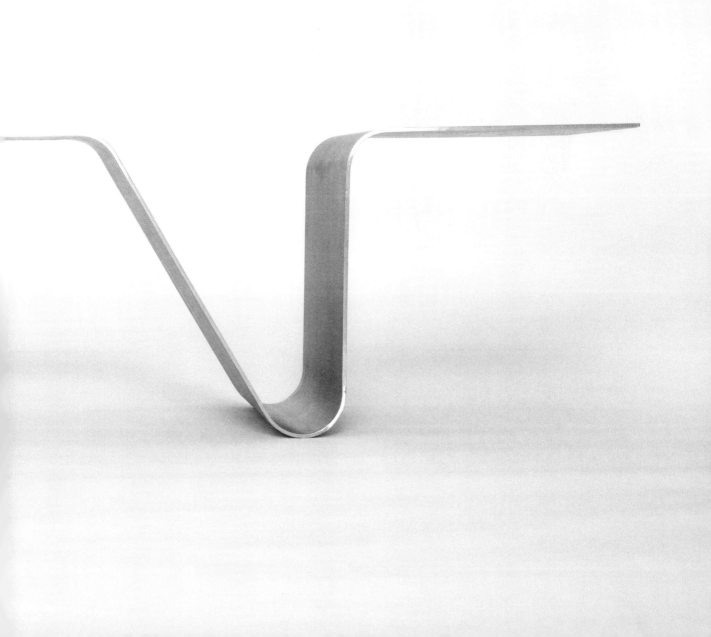

HI WAVE, 1998

'Sheila Hicks' way of originating from a raw material in her work was something that we could relate to, because that was the starting point for many of our designs. We wanted to find new applications for materials that came from outside the traditional furniture world. I had been researching technical textiles and was particularly interested in the textiles used for sails. A sail is never a single piece of textile; it is made of several different materials sewn together, and there was this particular kind used in light sails that struck me as both very durable and beautiful. So there was no sketch; the material was the starting point for the design, and then through experiments I reached the idea of using it for a lamp.' -Ilkka Suppanen

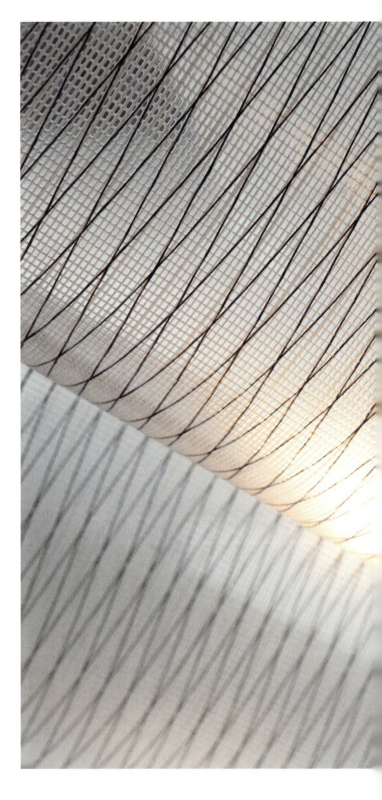

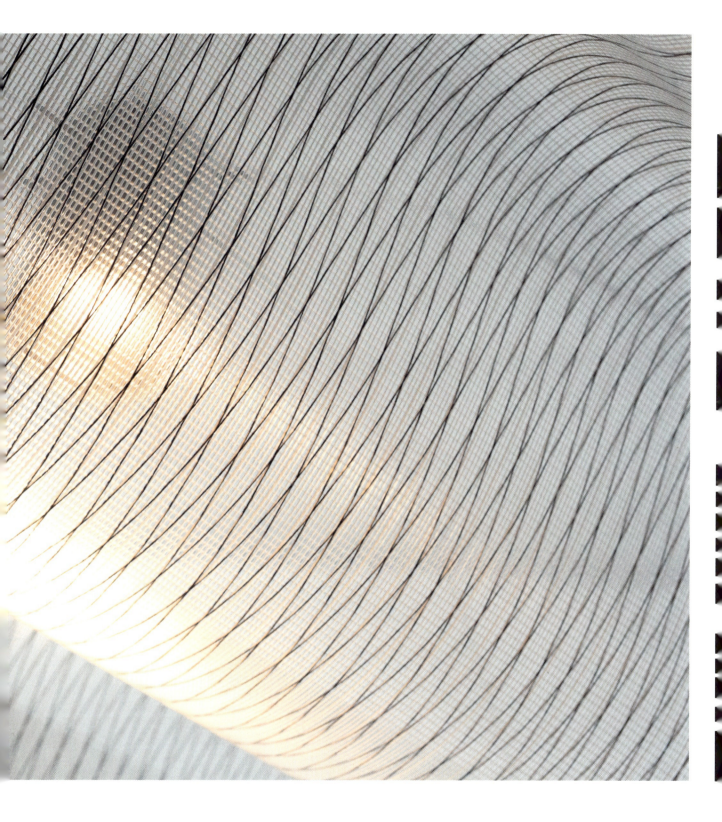

THE OFFICE

1. Godnatt Sverige! [Good Night Sweden!]. 1992. *Dagens Industri*. August 25th.
2. Elmbrant, Björn. 2005. *Dansen Runt Guldkalven: så förändrades Sverige av Börsbubblan* [The Dance Around the Golden Calf: How Sweden was changed by the Stock Market Bubble]. Atlas, 22.
3. Britton, Claes. 1999. Digital Frontier. *Stockholm New*. Issue 7, 46.
4. Conners Petersen, Leila. 1998. The Wired World Atlas. *Wired Magazine*. January 11th.

'Good Night Sweden!' was written in capital letters on the front page of the Swedish financial newspaper *Dagens Industri* on August 25th, 1992.[1] Just like Finland, Sweden had been crippled by a financial crisis during the first part of the 1990s. This had badly affected homeowners and small businesses due to a record high interest rate, brought on by deregulations of the financial market, and a weak Swedish currency—both countries would however end the decade on a record high.

In 1994 the first widely used web browser *Netscape* was launched, and 'when the American start-up was introduced on the Nasdaq stock exchange the following year, it surged like a rocket and made "IT" (information technology) companies something to be taken seriously'.[2] The introduction of software such as *Netscape* and *Windows 95* for PC computers popularised internet—making the Christmas gift of the year in Sweden in 1996 *The Internet Package* which contained everything you needed to get online. The computers, as Ilkka Terho had put it, no longer solely belonged to the geeks; average people started using it for e-mailing and soon also for shopping. Companies began to feel nervous because the future was coming. Few knew what it meant, but many were rushing to establish a presence on the internet, at any cost. Young people who could program a website became high in demand and some dropped out of school to start their own business, or started to work for a company that sold IT services such as Spray (1995) in Sweden and Netmill (1996) in Finland. The possibilities that opened up with smarter mobile phones and the sophistication of the internet, generated a tsunami of business ideas, and this creative atmosphere attracted eager venture capitalists who wanted to re-create the success of *Netscape*.

Nokia (1865) in Finland and its competitor Ericsson (1876) in Sweden—two telecommunications companies with more than 100 year old roots—had enabled residents in both countries to become some of the most connected people on the planet. By early 1999, the Swedish lifestyle magazine *Stockholm New* reported that there were approximately 700 'web companies' in Stockholm, nearly all of them established since 1996. In New York, that number was 1200.[3] The ongoing internet boom worked on a global level, but one of its definite centres was in the north, and for a while, the world media flocked here to study this exotic landscape up close, to get a handle on how technology had become a natural part of these cultures.

'Scandinavians and Icelanders seem to survive the long winter nights on communications technology more than on herring and akvavit. Throughout the Baltic nations and along the North Sea, there are more Internet hosts and cell phones per person than almost anywhere on the planet. To dine out or pub crawl in cities like Stockholm (often referred to as the centre of the Net in Europe) and Helsinki (where three in four residents pack a mobile phone) is to be in constant communicado with friends, maître d's, and taxis', wrote Leila Conners Petersen for *Wired Magazine* in 1998.[4]

108–109
Snowcrash fair stand at IFF Köln, 2000

5. Lindén, Carl-Gustav. 2015. *Nokia och Finland: rapport från de galna åren* [Nokia and Finland: a report from the crazy years]. Schildts & Söderströms, 165
6. 2000. Shining Stockholm. *Newsweek*. June 2nd.
7. Elmbrant, Björn. 2005. *Dansen Runt Guldkalven: så förändrades Sverige av Börsbubblan* [The Dance Around the Golden Calf: How Sweden was changed by the Stock Market Bubble]. Atlas, 125.
8. Weil, Robert. 2000. Du ska inte blanda dig [You shall not blend]. *Dagens Industri*. April 8th, 35.

Approaching the new millennium, everyone from the person on the street to super heroes like Neo in *The Matrix* (1999) had a Nokia phone, Nokia was now the leading mobile phone manufacturer and one of the five most valuable trademarks in the world.[5] Swedish IT company Framfab had at the same time become Europe's largest IT consultancy company and the third largest in the world.[6] Anything or anyone related to IT seemed to be able to turn water into wine, and this was confirmed by the curves on the stock market and stories in the newspapers. It was a modern day gold rush and regular people eventually also joined in and invested their savings. But just when people and companies could exhale again—after it stood clear that the 'millennium bug' or 'Y2K' had not scrambled the world's computer systems—overrated IT companies that could not deliver on the ideas they had sold started to crash, and what had been called 'the internet bubble' began to deflate. As the Swedish journalist Björn Elmbrant put it: 'If *Netscape*'s introduction to the stock market in 1995 had been the catalyst for the money from venture capitalists to flow, then the crash of Swedish online retailer of fashionable goods boo.com in the spring of 2000, became symbolic in the opposite meaning'.[7] In these fast and turbulent times Robert Weil, the founder of Proventus, shared his thoughts in a column in *Dagens Industri*, where he showed both excitement as well as a call for restraint:

'Distribution and communication technology is being developed with furious speed. The knowledge to utilise them and the presentation of what is jointly happening in culture and industry, becomes more exciting than ever. The vision of the future is changing faster than ever. But the commotion on the stock market and the IT craze is rushing forward faster than the reality. Take it easy! Gather your thoughts! The future is dynamic, even though the present is hysterical.'[8]

Snowcrash had been successfully launched as a new company in the beginning of 1999. And being on the threshold to a new millennium—with everything that was happening in technology—Robert Weil felt that they were in a exceptional position to fully explore what that meant, and therefore initiated talks with the young economist and entrepreneur Andreas Murray. He was the co-founder of the Swedish advertising and design company Futurniture (1993), which very much adhered to an IT community where technology, economy and design cross-pollinated each other. In the beginning of 2000, he would bring a strain of that culture with him into Snowcrash as its new CEO. Snowcrash would from now on seek to innovate not only through its objects, but also as a company.

'These were exceptional times. With the new technology that emerged, which no one at the time could predict would so fundamentally change the fabric of our society, also lay a challenge in how to create a company that best could utilise it. So I very much saw my part in Snowcrash as a search for a new business model. Robert had not

WEBSITE

'The site was to be ready for their show in Milan in the spring of 1999, and we were a small team working on it at the digital agency Mindworks Oy (Ltd). We were used to working dynamically but this time our setup was almost too risky - considering that remote work in those days was still in its early stages. I was managing the project while birdwatching on the Åland Islands; programmer Mikko Karvonen was at the office in downtown Helsinki; while the designer Niko was in Kathmandu.' -Mika Ilari Koskinen. 'I was working on the site in Photoshop on my laptop, a PowerBook G3, while sitting in a restaurant lit only by candles, as the power was lost nearly every evening around 6pm. Later, in a hotel in Bangkok, I used my yellow Nokia 5110 with a 9.6Kbps bandwidth to transfer the data in time.' -Niko Punin

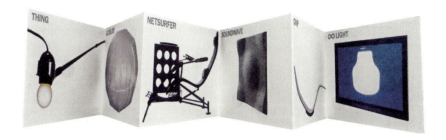

GRAPHIC PROFILE

'I was working on the company's graphic profile between 1999-2002, and sought to create a profile that was leaning towards "tech" without feeling cold. I brought out a somewhat warm metallic nuance in the typography where applicable. Print was still an important part of the identity of a company then, so I worked on creating a product folder which presented the collection, letterheads, business cards and invitations.' -Lars Fuhre

9. Murray, Andreas. 2020. Telephone interview March 27th.
10. Murray, Andreas. 2020. Stockholm 2018. Interview May 14th.
11. Bluetooth. *Understanding Bluetooth Range.* https://www.bluetooth.com/learn-about-bluetooth/bluetooth-technology/range/ (2020-04-02)
12. Tuck, Andrew. 2000. The ICD+ jacket: Slip into my office, please. *The Independent.* September 4th. https://www.independent.co.uk/news/business/analysis-and-features/the-icd-jacket-slip-into-my-office-please-694074.html (2020-04-02)
13. *Snowcrash.* 2000. Snowcrash. Press release. April 14th.

given me an assignment with instructions; instead we had a continuous creative dialogue and I felt free to explore.'[9]

The Snowcrash office moved from Växjö in the south of Sweden to Tulegatan in central Stockholm and Andreas Murray began to hire the right competence to help him build a design company for the 21st century.

'Snowcrash did not have its own production or any established distribution network, so we had the opportunity to develop new solutions in many traditional areas. Early on we explored e-commerce but of course no one at the time had taken this step in the furniture business so we did not understand how easy or difficult it could be. Many different ideas were discussed, and simultaneously we were looking for ways to utilise all this new technology with design.'[10]

Netsurfer, *Globlow* and *Jack in the Box* were objects which in different ways had incorporated electronic hardware, and it was now high time to explore if the same could not be done with software. In 1999 the Swedish telecommunications company Ericsson was among the first to successfully develop and release a new technology called Bluetooth, which meant wireless, short range communication between electric devices.[11] Andreas Murray engaged the product developer Gustaf Rosell, who had knowledge in this field, to work out a technical concept for furniture using Bluetooth. The fashion industry had already explored ideas about wearable technology, which in spirit bordered on the wireless theme, and in the beginning of 2000 the *ICD+* jacket was released. This was the result of a collaboration between Levi's and the Dutch electronics firm Philips. Aimed at 'urban nomads', it enabled the wearer to easily control different digital gear, such as mobile phones and Mp3 players.[12] A sample of this jacket was also bought and used as inspiration, and in the hands of Snowcrash, the humble desk was destined to be elevated from mere furniture to a wireless connection hub.

'It is actually quite natural that a desk, which in the open office landscape constitutes the centre of the work place, functions as a gateway or bridge towards the internet. In my opinion this is even more relevant than hooking up a fridge ...in the long run we will see even more of the technical functions that today are placed within the walls, floor and ceiling of the office, transferred to systems of furniture', Gustaf Rosell later stated in the press release.[13] The table, designed by Teppo Asikainen and Ilkka Terho, got the name *Broadway* and was one of several new products being developed for presentation at Salone del Mobile in Milan, 2000.

Ever since a contract had been written between the originators behind Snowcrash and Proventus Design, the team at Valvomo, Timo Salli and Ilkka Suppanen, had been engaged on a freelance basis while also working for other clients. Andreas Murray now hired Ilkka Suppanen as creative director for Snowcrash, and collaborations with new designers were established. Robert Weil proposed a meeting with

14. Levy, Arik. 2019. Telephone interview October 7th.
15. Ljungberg, Ulrika. 2020. Telephone interview October 20th.
16. Hamilton L., William. 2000. Breaking, not making the mould. *The New York Times*. April 20th.

Israeli designer Arik Levy, who had recently made scenography for the Batsheva Dance Company, of which Proventus had been a supporter since 1998. After a meaningful meeting in Arik Levy's studio in Paris, he partook in creative discussions in Stockholm and two designs from his studio, the conceptual lamps *Infinite Light* and *Thing*, were added to the Snowcrash collection.

'Snowcrash consisted of a good and dynamic group of people. I had previously seen them in Milan and they clearly had a different ideology from the rest of the industry. What was different was the courage and approach to design; it was completely detached from tradition and I think that was an advantage. We were also given great suport from the management, which was fundamental for us to explore new areas together.'[14]

In January 2000, not long after Arik Levy had joined, Andreas Murray hired the Swedish interior architect Ulrika Ljungberg. She had been living in Italy for eight years, studying at Istituto Europeo di Design in Milan and Fabrica in Treviso, and worked with legends in the Italian radical design movement such as Alessandro Guerriero. Ljungberg knew Milan, spoke the language, and was immediately engaged in planning for the big Snowcrash launch during Salone del Mobile. Snowcrash was to present its upgraded, slightly more wireless collection, with new works such as the table *Broadway*; *Globlow LED* which could be controlled with a mobile phone; and the acoustic panel *Soundwave Swell*. But it was far from certain if all of them would be ready in time for the show in April.

'The playful, conceptual approach to design that I had learned in Italy, with genuine ideas that went beyond mere aesthetics, was something I also saw in the Snowcrash products. And everything we did until the end with the collection and events, aimed at creating a joyous and communal spirit between people. After finding a beautiful space at Spazio Nicole Tomas in the Brera area, the challenge was to create a memorable experience that reflected the organic and animated feeling in the products, even if we did not get to show the new designs. I created a skin coloured floor and reception space, with a room within the room made out of white textiles, that had an infinity perspective. Lamps shifted between a warm and a cold light—it was like a living technological organism that pulsated to the Snowcrash soundtrack by Mika Vainio.'[15]

The exhibition manifested Andreas Murray's vision of a new design company for a new age, which he also underlined in an interview with *The New York Times*: 'Why produce things as they did in the 1950s, when we live in the 21st century? Beautiful things that communicate with whom? Ten thousand, 50.000 people in the world? It is nice to be here, looking at what others are doing, but for us, the consumer electronics show in Las Vegas would be a better place for our next exhibition'.[16]

Snowcrash was by now synonymous with the cutting edge in the

INFINITE LIGHT, 1999

The original design by Arik Levy, was a one hour film of a light bulb.
You put the VHS into the video player and your TV becomes a lamp
that you can dim or make brighter by using the TV remote control.
Later it was digitalised so it also could be projected. As it said
in the Snowcrash product folder 'While the beauty of the *Infinite
light* is the idea of an immaterial light with an infinite life, the
image of the light bulb links future technology and the history of
electricity.'

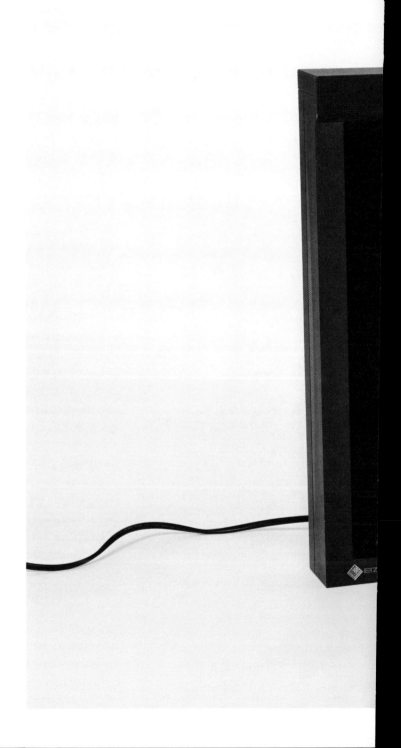

THING, 1999

'*Thing* is a conceptual readymade. A light bulb at the end of a collapsible, telescopic metal rod that costs nearly nothing. It was a new centre of gravity and it brought light to spaces in architecture where there had not been any light before. You could lean it in a corner, use it as a hanging light fixture, or hold it out into a dark empty void and let the light sink down, and then reel it in according to need.' -Arik Levy

17. Budd, Christopher. 2001. The Office: 1950 to the Present. Antonelli, Paola (editor). *Workspheres: Design and Contemporary Work Styles*. New York: Museum of Modern Art / Thames and Hudson, 34.
18. Ando, Haj. *Chiat/Day NY in the late 90s*. http://www.hajando.com/chiat-nyc (2020-05-10)

press, and Andreas Murray and his team aimed to push further into unchartered digital areas—but everybody knew that they needed commercial successes to stay alive. A more traditional analysis of Snowcrash's reason for being had also been made, and the opportunity lay in furnishing the emerging 'in-between' spaces in the office environment.

The theme at the Alternative Office Expo where *Netsurfer* had been shown in 1996 was, 'Where you sit is where you work', and the international ad campaign from Canon that was running hot at the same time said 'Work where you want'. The workplace as people knew it became more fluid in the 1990s. With the internet and office equipment becoming smaller, cheaper and easier to use, work could be done from home. Flexible work stations and working from a distance freed up increasingly expensive office space, and companies not willing to pay rent for empty desks took the opportunity to shrink a size or two to cut costs.

'An emphasis was placed on less-hierarchical, more-nimble organisations that focused on interaction and communication, and on the increasing importance of social connections.'[17] The new office of the American advertising company Chiat/Day in New York—designed in 1995 by Gaetano Pesce—stood as a prime example of this new change and was widely publicised for its groundbreaking layout without fixed work stations, and for its playful interior. It was also criticised for being over the top—prompting a former employee to state about one of its rooms: 'It's like being inside a small child's stomach just after they have eaten a bottle of Flintstone vitamins'.[18] In any case, it had officially shown that an office did not have to look like an office, and that the latest episode of *Seinfeld* did not have to be discussed at the designated water cooler area anymore. A new generation of workers had also entered the office, not necessarily straight out of a Douglas Coupland novel, but nonetheless employees who considered casual Fridays to be something invented by dinosaurs. Established companies had to re-adjust their interiors to become more informal and fun in order to attract this young and tech savvy work force. And for all the new tech start-up companies that needed an office 'yesterday', there were simply no rules for how an interior could look.

The objects in the Snowcrash exhibition of 1997 had laid the foundation for a typology which was in tune with this change, and new and old additions to the Snowcrash collection were now being packaged to be marketed and sold together. To help Snowcrash shape the collection and communicate their designs, Robert Weil suggested that they engage the British writer and curator Jane Withers.

'When Snowcrash landed in Milan it drew on different cultural references and offered a new vision of how the next generation could be living and working, collaborating and creating, and of course surfing and gaming. Like its Dutch contemporaries Droog, it was raw, poetic and conceptually daring, and courted attention. The horizontal slouch

GLOBLOW LED, 2000

'We were eager to do something that was new and "special" and since we had already made a lamp that came to life with a fan, it felt perfectly natural to make it even more interactive. LEDs were rare on the mass-market and quite expensive, but we managed to get some from a company in Helsinki that made advertising signs. We put the components together with the help of a friend, Jari Lehtinen, who often worked with artists on projects with electronics; the circuitboard functioned as the base for the construction of the whole lamp. We glued the ripstop nylon, and soldered the LEDs onto the circuitboard, then a separate transformer got the right voltage to it. With the first prototype, we got a Finnish SIM card wired to the circuitboard so you could send a text message with your phone which would then change the colour of the light. So when demonstrating the lamp at the design-week in Milan, you sent a text message to Finland to change the light in Italy. In later prototypes we of course experimented with WiFi.' -Vesa Hinkola

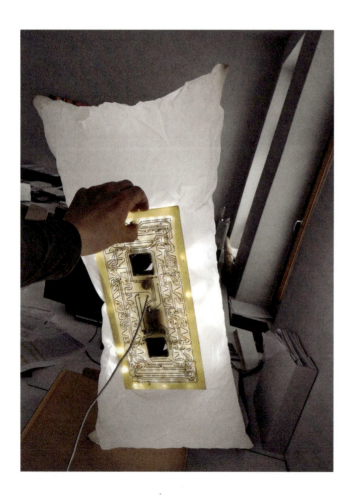

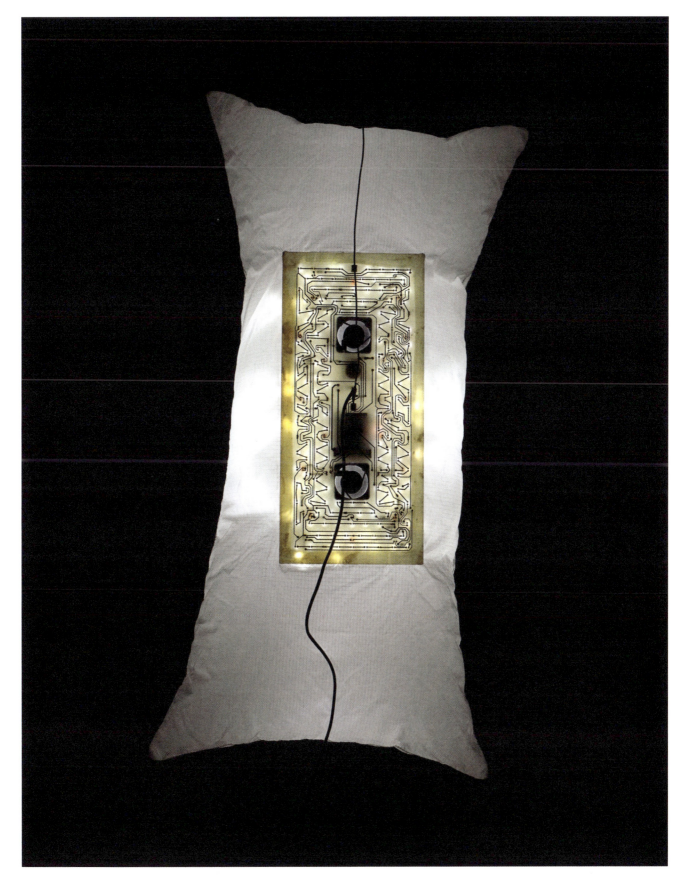

19. Withers, Jane. 2018. Skype interview September 26th
20. Murray, Andreas. 2020. Stockholm 2018. Interview May 14th.
21. Mårtensson, Ulrika. 2018. Telephone interview June 1st.
22. Murray, Andreas. 2020. Stockholm 2018. Interview May 14th.

of Snowcrash loungers and inflatables was designed to equip a new breed of nomadic cyber surfers. It was optimistic and as much about creating an image as functionality. A deliberate challenge to the staid and grey, corporate and hierarchical world of most workplace design. There were also interesting products that focussed on less visible areas such as the *Soundwave* panels to elegantly tackle acoustics in open plan spaces.'[19]

'Our focus was to create objects for the in-between spaces away from the work desks, where people socialised and worked, and new solutions for light and acoustics were needed there. The acoustic panels in the *Soundwave* series had basically created a whole new market on their own, and naturally we continued to explore that area with other designs.'[20]

One of these new products would be made with the Swedish architect and textile designer Ulrika Mårtensson, who was creating textiles with sound absorbing properties at Konstfack University of Arts, Crafts and Design in Stockholm. During two years Ulrika Mårtensson had developed these textiles in collaboration with Kinnasand, and the collection, entitled *Stiller,* was her graduation project. While on an exchange programme in Helsinki before graduation in the spring of 2000, Ulrika Mårtensson met Ilkka Suppanen, who suggested that her research in this field could continue at Snowcrash.

'I was working on these textiles around the same time as Snowcrash were making their acoustic panels, so it made perfect sense for us to work together. It was a very visionary company and I felt that they represented an exciting conceptual design which I had not seen before. At Snowcrash we continued to experiment with different types of textiles and fibres in workshops, in order to make a new product that could become a part of their collection.'[21]

'Using light and tactile materials like felt and textiles was a way to create a human expression in office interiors, and since there were no telling how the new technology would affect our habits and lifestyles, any shape or size was imaginable to us. It spoke the same language as Monica Förster's *Cloud*—from the first moment I saw it, it was just obvious to me that it was a Snowcrash meeting room. There was never a question of whether a meeting room could actually look or function like that.'[22]

Andreas Murray had been intrigued by an exhibition architecture made by the young Swedish designer Monica Förster, which consisted of an inflated room, and he had proposed to Monica Förster that it be brought into Snowcrash as a new project. This very act was an example of the kind of atmosphere that was cultivated and valued at Snowcrash, following the same open-mindedness towards aesthetics, technology and materials that had been manifested in the exhibition in 1997. Luckily, this is also something that was respected by its owner, who saw Snowcrash as a prime example of a company where art and technology could come together.

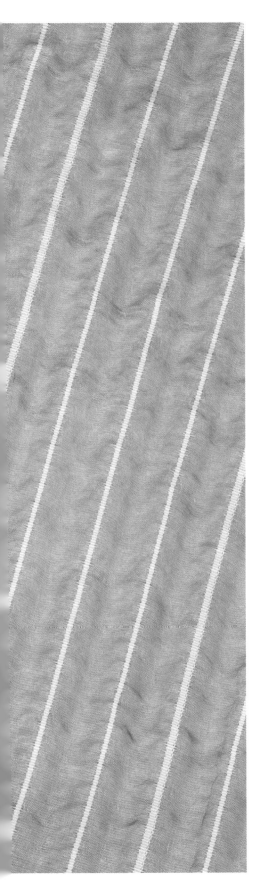

THE SOUND SOLUTION COLLECTION

'You would think that drapes had always been used to give good acoustics in interiors, but people forget that they basically disappeared with modernism because they were deemed unhygienic. While working as an interior architect, before I studied textile design, I noticed that there was an unattended gap on the market when it came to acoustic products. With Maria Lomholt as project leader and Sheila Hicks as artistic advisor, I made a lot of tests with different fibres and ways of weaving them. Sound-absorbing textiles have their limitations; there is an intricate equation that needs to be solved so that they are not too heavy and have the right density, etc. In the 1990s, textiles were supposed to hang straight and be kind of discrete. So I made five designs that offered maximum sound absorption based on their specific character. One of these was transparent, something that basically did not exist on the market, but we succeeded.'
-Ulrika Mårtensson

23. Hicks, Sheila. 2020. Telephone interview August 13th.
24. Hicks, Sheila. 2018. Skype interview May 14th.
25. *Exhibition at MoMa Features Innovative Design Solutions for the Workplace of the Near Future.* 2001. The Museum of Modern Art, New York. Press release January.

Still images from private movie of Snowcrash installation in the *Workspheres* exhibition at MoMA, 2001

In the mid 1990s, Robert Weil had appointed the American textile artist Sheila Hicks as chairman of the board at Kinnasand. Sheila Hicks had an extensive knowledge of merging the arts with industry, having worked on several continents in various industrial settings for decades. The scope of projects ranged from commissioned art works and instigating artisanal projects in developing countries, to designing furniture fabrics for Knoll and textile bas-relief panels for Air France's Boeing 747s. As a matter of fact, Proventus Design had been exposed to her work when she exhibited at the Artek Gallery in Helsinki and at Nordiska Kompaniet department store in Stockholm in 1966. Robert Weil asked Sheila Hicks to be an advisor to Snowcrash and she quickly saw that the collection embodied a rare quality—it did not automatically adhere to a familiar design language. The designers' inventiveness and use of materials attracted her, and Sheila Hicks's future involvement in the creative process was to make sure that this sensitivity was not lost in Snowcrash's strive to reach the international market and become industrialised.

'They were inventing new shapes with noble materials, that were restrained in a way so that they never became vulgar. The objects were aesthetically tuned to function, elegant and beyond, which made them strong enough to be in a space between different art forms. You could say that the designers were thinking of Le Corbusier at the same time as they were thinking of Brâncuși or Noguchi. This is interesting, because we look at those objects more innocently. It has to do with taking a leap from the natural world to the technical, where hard relinquishes space and allows the soft part to enter the same stage. When you can incorporate something so beautiful that a person does not know whether to sit or sleep on it or merely contemplate it as sculpture, you have succeeded.'[23]

Besides being active in reviewing prototyping stages, Sheila Hicks also participated in strategic meetings: 'At the meetings I was a good listener. When different ideas were presented I tried to see how they fitted into a larger context. I had the benefit of being an outsider and therefore could also give honest opinions without worrying about crossing any comfort zones—my experience is that people benefit if you tell them your true reactions. I also went with them to MoMA when they exhibited there. I think that was a new high for everyone, and rightly so.'[24]

Having only existed as a company for two years, with a collection that in most parts could be described as prototypes made to order, Snowcrash had received an invitation from the curator Paola Antonelli at the Museum of Modern Art (MoMA) in New York, to be a part of the exhibition *Workspheres*. The exhibition opened in February 2001 and featured 'innovative design solutions for the workplace of the near future'[25], as it said in the press release, and here parts of the Snowcrash collection were on display in the presence of office furniture giants such as Hayworth, Knoll and Herman Miller. After the exhibition ended,

26. Antonelli, Paola. 2020. Email August 17th.
27. Murray, Andreas. 2020. Stockholm 2018. Interview May 14th.

the products *Soundwave Swell*, *Globlow* and *Feltboxes* also became a part of MoMA's collection.

'My office at MoMA is to this day covered in felt tiles that originally came from *Workspheres*. The exhibition talked about the way people worked at a very interesting time, in the waning months of the dotcom boom. People were inebriated with the offerings of new technology, which allowed for brand new ways of working that demanded brand new typologies of office/non-office furniture, such as a seemingly floating chaise lounge with a computer served as a food tray—or as a spaceship control deck—clearly for a pioneering tech entrepreneur. Both the launch pad and the acoustic insulation tiles came from Snowcrash.'[26]

At Snowcrash, the hope was that participation in *Workspheres* would be their ticket into the American market. But Snowcrash was instead expanding in another time zone, namely at their office in Stockholm. In the beginning of 2001, Snowcrash posted a half page ad in the biggest newspaper in Sweden—in which they were looking to fill a number of new positions—and by the time of the exhibition at MoMA, the company had grown from a handful of people to over 20 employees. The new colleagues had very competitive backgrounds, coming from companies such as Ikea, Saab and IBM, and the ambition to scale up was obvious, but by now the explorative no-rules management approach had begun to take its toll.

'Based on discussions with Robert I had the freedom to create my own work frame and I also wished that for the people I employed, so they could invent new ways of working in relation to IT. But from the start, maybe both my description as a CEO and also the directions I gave to my coworkers, should have been clearer. I had left my coworkers without specific goals and budget which resulted in a creative chaos, and we had reached a point where I realised we needed fixed guidelines to move onto an industrial level.'[27]

Andreas Murray stayed on, but took a step back in favour of a reconstruction of the management. The same person that would run Snowcrash would also be the CEO of Proventus Design—which in 2000 had changed its name to Art & Technology by Proventus. The Italian engineer and entrepreneur Pio Barone Lumaga was headhunted for the position and it was considered a dream recruitment. Pio Barone Lumaga spoke four languages, had a doctorate in environmental engineering and had previously been the managing partner of Studio de Lucchi and the CEO of Danese in Italy. At the time of the offer, Pio Barone Lumaga operated a Think tank in Los Angeles, and having accepted, he sold his company and the house in California and moved to Sweden in August 2001.

'I met Robert Weil and was inspired by his commitment to culture and ability to choose companions on his journey. I loved the companies' Swedish Finnish heritage and received a threefold assignment: make Snowcrash grow, place Artek on the international map, and find

SOUNDWAVE ACOUSTIC SERIES; SWELL, 1999

This product was first shown at the international furniture and interiors fair IMM in Köln, January 2000. It came to life when Valvomo got the assignment to design the restaurant Pravda (2000) in Helsinki, which was located door to door with the Artek store on Södra Esplanaden. 'There were hard surfaces everywhere in the restaurant so we wanted something for the wall that could absorb sound. I had imagined it to be like a 3D wallpaper, but we just could not find the right product for it. The previous year, I had visited a factory in Lahti, where I was given a piece of the felt used to make the interiors for cars and asked if I could do something with that. So then it all came together. I proposed the idea of *Soundwave* to Ragne Bogholt, who recognised that this was a good time to invest in a mould since we had both the restaurant project and the booth in Köln coming up.' -Teppo Asikainen

SOUNDWAVE ACOUSTIC SERIES; SCRUNCH, 2001

The shape was first drawn up in CAD software, but feeling that the digital tool could not give the right balance of soft and hard, Teppo Asikainen instead wrinkled a physical aluminium plate by hand.

THE OFFICE

28. Lumaga Barone, Pio. 2018. Skype interview September 29th.
29. Ljungberg, Ulrika. 2020. Telephone interview October 20th.
30. Tham, Bolle and Videgård, Martin. Stockholm 2019. Interview September 24th.
31. Tham, Bolle and Videgård, Martin. Stockholm 2019. Interview September 24th.
32. Tham, Bolle and Videgård, Martin. Stockholm 2019. Interview September 24th.

a new soul for Kinnasand. Each firm, a complexity in itself, needed to evolve, Artek had a beautiful classic collection designed many decades before by Aino and Alvar Aalto; Kinnasand's respected curtain business, with a great heritage as supplier to the royal house, required a new playing field; and Snowcrash, a fresh design experiment, called for production and a commercial structure.'[28]

When Pio Barone Lumaga was on his way into Snowcrash, Snowcrash was in the process of getting a new office, in part because they had outgrown their former premises on Tulegatan and because they needed to lead by example. They had found an old warehouse from the 1940s on Textilvägen in a developing area south of the city called Hammarby. Here they took over a 1183 square metre floor which was to be turned into their combined office and showroom. The move meant that Snowcrash had the opportunity to put theory in to practice and physically become the office they had envisioned. As a foundation, Ulrika Ljunggren made a study of some of the employees' behavioural patterns in the office and conducted interviews with everyone to map out specific needs and functions.

'The idea was to have a set of rooms with different shapes and functions so people could choose what suited them and their task best; a range from formal to casual—from the open office landscape where you were a part of a community, to a soundproofed booth for solitude. It was vital that we maintained the creative atmosphere that we had built up at Tulegatan, and we wanted our new office to feel more like a work in progress, that it was in constant movement.'[29]

The newly founded Swedish architecture practice Tham & Videgård Hansson got the assignment, and together with Ulrika Ljungberg at Snowcrash they completed the project in 100 days.

'Compared to how office furniture looked like at that time, Snowcrash was an odd bird that made you think and question the norm. They were quite aware of how they wanted to be represented as a brand, and had started to build a community where all the employees were part of this forward motion. Our role was to make a physical interpretation of that.'[30]

'We also saw things in Snowcrash that spoke to us, because we ourselves were reevaluating traditional patterns and behaviours, such as life in a home—do we need this particular set of rooms with predetermined functions, or can we change the spatiality based on needs, and so on.'[31]

'The ideas for alternative ways of living presented in the 80s by the British practice Future Systems really came to life around this time. In general there was a shift in architecture from postmodernism in the 80s, recession and a lot of theorising, to this moment where there was an expectancy to represent and also practice something new—but what that was, was unknown. There was a shared belief in the future which was exhilarating, and that feeling also influenced the aesthetics.'[32]

33. Tham, Bolle and Videgård, Martin. Stockholm 2019. Interview September 24th.

'The Snowcrash collection was very dynamic—it was light, mobile, changeable—and combined with a scenario of where Snowcrash would be in the future, made us think of how it could change over time based on needs. Our whole programme rested on the idea that as little as possible was permanently built, so we made a structure with a glass wall that acted like an amoeba that easily could be altered, moved or taken down altogether.'[33]

Despite the seemingly flawless line-up of creative competence, experience and know how that now was gathered under one roof, it would as it so happened be the latter of the architects' scenarios that played out. Snowcrash would be taken down altogether before it reached commercial success.

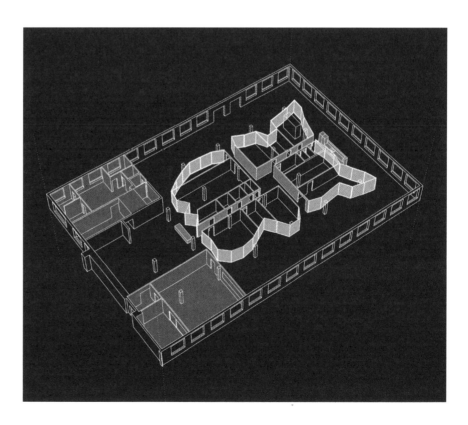

Overview of the new Snowcrash office

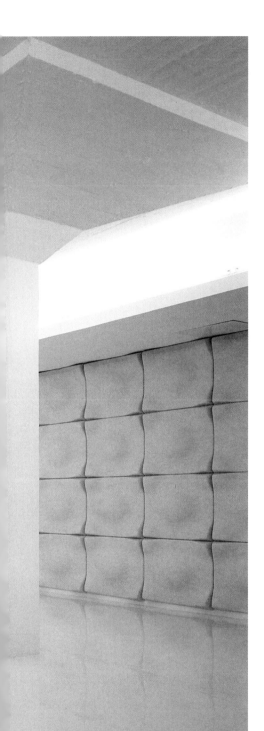

THE OFFICE, 2001

'We wanted the office to have a transparency in all regards. To that end we applied a pattern of small dots on the glass walls outlining the rooms, which were spaced to allow light to flow into the rooms but prevent the possibility of reading anyone's lips. The reception area functioned as an exhibition space where we displayed prototypes so co-workers and visitors could see and give us feedback on our progress.' -Ulrika Ljungberg. The Snowcrash office was awarded first prize for interior/environmental design by the short lived, but prestigious *Core Design Awards*, in 2001.

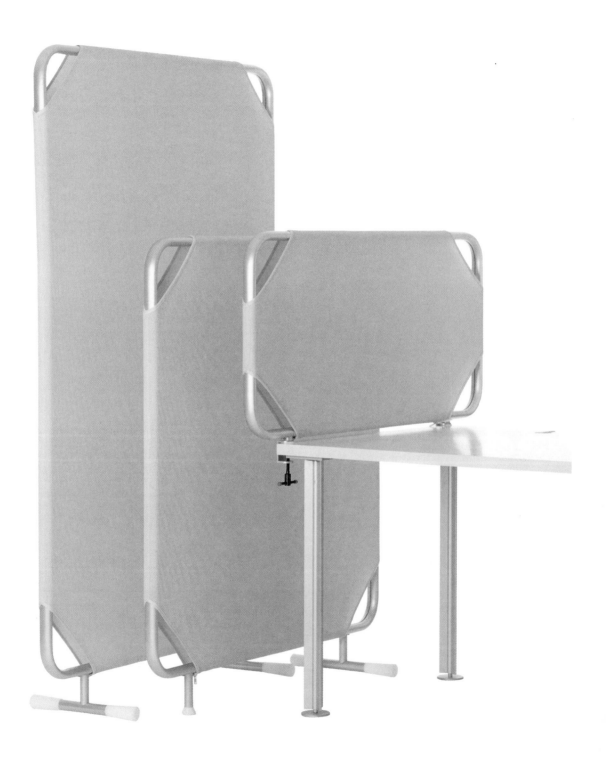

LOCO - Ilkka Suppanen, 2001

LOCO PROTOTYPE, 2001

ADDAPT, 2001

'A product for the non-territorial workplace that accommodated a new type of lifestyle. People started to go to the gym before coming in to work, and then after work they went straight to a social function. So it was a portable filing system, clip on bags, for all these different purposes.' -Arik Levy

FELTBOX, 2000

Following a product brief in the 'storage' category, Markus Nevalainen and Kari Sivonen designed *Feltbox*, and prototypes were shown, in the *Workspheres* exhibition at MoMA in 2001. Made with the same manufacturing technique as the *Soundwave* panels - moulded in a felt material - the boxes help absorb and reduce noise. The boxes can be stacked into, or on top of each other, using the lid, which also serves as a tray. *Feltbox* gives the classic 'bankers box' a much needed upgrade and is a part of a larger storage system that has the nomadic work style in mind. When leaving the office in the evening, you can put your belongings in the box and store it on a shelf. When picking your box up in the morning, you can either carry it or put it on a trolley and roll down to your preferred workstation for the day. A shelf system based on the Feltbox concept, was developed at the same time.

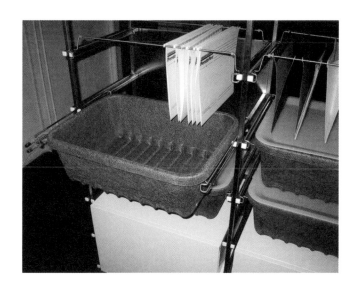

NETSURFER, 1995

Nearly 200 copies of Teppo Asikainen and Ilkka Terho's *Netsurfer*, was
produced and manufactured by Snowcrash in Sweden between 1999 and 2002.

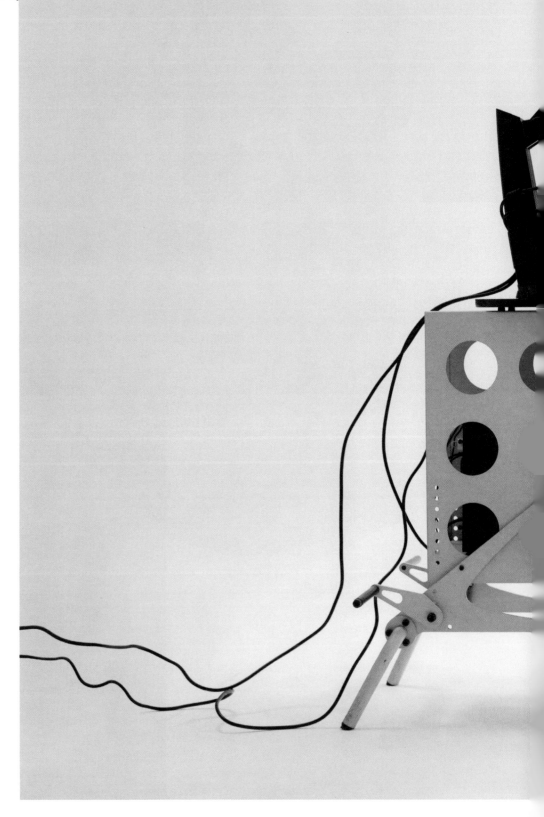

SNOWCRASH ON ICE

1. Lancken von der, Charlotte. 2019. Telephone interview September 24th
2. Andersson, Hans och Svensson, Johan. Stockholm 2020. Interview February 18th.
3. Andersson, Hans och Svensson, Johan. Stockholm 2020. Interview February 18th.

'As students at Konstfack University of Arts, Crafts and Design we were always reaching outwards, constantly discussing form and function, and Snowcrash was a hot topic. The general feeling was that design was standing still and that Droog and Snowcrash were fun, uplifting and thought provoking companies that represented something new. I was doing my third year of the Industrial Design programme when I got an internship there—a kind of dream position for many of us. I worked on different projects and their level of technical quality was very impressive. Also, the atmosphere at the office in Hammarby was happy and open minded—it was a great experience.'[1]

There was full activity at the new Snowcrash office. With new leadership and colleagues, everybody was hard at work; several new ideas for how to expand the collection had been instigated; and there had even been talks about a possible collaboration with the renowned institution MIT (Massachusetts Institute of Technology) in the USA, to try out new technology. Wellbeing in the office environment continued to be a focal point, and having started to tackle an invisible health problem such as sound pollution, the conversation continued about cleaner air, and how air purifiers could potentially be integrated into furniture. An alternative approach to this issue was the traditional use of indoor plants. The French designer Andrée Putman (1925–2013) had made the interior at Pershing Hall Hotel (2001) in Paris, in which the botanist Patric Blanc had created a vertical garden. Being a friend of Andrée Putman, Robert Weil set up a meeting between Andreas Murray and Patric Blanc, and this sparked a new project at Snowcrash. Hans Andersson and Johan Svensson, who had worked together on product development and sourcing at Snowcrash since 2000, were asked to take a closer look at this.

'Andreas Murray had instigated this track at the office but what it would lead to was an open question. It was very interesting because this was an area and a technique that was foreign to us, so we had to do a lot of research. We started reading NASA's hand books on how to grow plants in space with hydroponics.'[2]

'At Snowcrash there were many discussion about what you really do at the office. What are working hours and what happens between ordinary activities? This generated topics such as "sleep, eat and exercise at work", which were conceptually challenging and exciting. If the office is more like the place where you also live, then a a kitchen garden where you can grow your own food is relevant to look at in a metropolitan area. So having started with plants functioning as air purifiers, we ended up with an idea about modern ecology and design instead.'[3]

While some ideas and concepts were in early stages, others had reached completion. Monica Förster's *Cloud* had been fully developed and was ready to be launched at the Salone del Mobile in April, 2002.

'The exhibition room I had originally made was constructed with arches to maintain the shape while it was filled with air by a fan—a

152–153
Plant garden prototype

Experiments with a plant garden in the Snowcrash office, 2002

4. Förster, Monica. 2020. Telephone interview February 21st.
5. Repetto, Federico. 2018. Skype interview May 18th.
6. Levy, Arik. 2019. Telephone interview October 7th.
7. Andersson, Hans och Svensson, Johan. Stockholm 2020. Interview February 18th.

person who built hot air balloons had helped me to make it. At that stage I did not have a name for it and when it was taken down you moved it around on a trolley. After prototyping at Snowcrash, the shape and concept changed and we made it fit into a bag that you could carry over your shoulder. I was young and had only made one other design for production before, so when the press went crazy with *Cloud* in Milan, I was a bit taken by it. I was standing in a crowd one evening at Bar Basso and everyone was talking about *Cloud* but nobody knew that it was I who had done it—it felt a bit unreal.'[4]

Out of some 20 different brands that exhibited their latest products at the new space *La Pelota*, Snowcrash with its headliner *Cloud* became the definite showstopper. The previous year, Pio Barone Lumaga had brought in Federico Repetto, who had worked with major Italian brands such as Poltrona Frau, as the new marketing director for Artek and Snowcrash—and the launch in Milan was his first with the company.

'I remember that people almost freaked out when they saw Monica's *Cloud* in our booth in Milan. We received so much press. In general we did not have to spend a penny on advertising for Snowcrash, which I understood was normal for them, but I discovered that we had other problems, such as delivering what we sold. When I started we had quickly engaged my international network and opened up 10–15 new markets in the first six months; I was eager to do this because these avant garde products had not been distributed before. At Artek the production, logistics and stocking were flawless, while with Snowcrash it was a challenge since there was no structure in place; there was this disconnection between the prototype and the product line.'[5]

Few design companies had managed to build up the kind of reputation and image that Snowcrash had in the same period of time. But it had come at the expense of fundamental structural issues that no longer could be ignored.

'I came to Stockholm regularly for a long time and I loved going there. Every day was full of discussions and confrontations that were very positive, constructive and which resulted in new ideas. It was a true melting pot where you met the possibility, the creative substance and also the willingness to do something different. But the world did not turn at the same speed as the ideas that were thrown around, and things never moved out of this experimental bubble to the industrial level, which was what Snowcrash needed and aimed for.'[6]

'As creative as the atmosphere was, it was frustrating at times because the design process never really closed. There was this constant input which meant that things did not leave the prototyping phase. One of the consequences of this was that we could not confirm on which level to put the production: made to order in small quantities, or large orders at big factories with more capacity.'[7]

Eva-Lott Lydholm, who had joined the company in 2000 working with international sales, experienced no problem in explaining to her

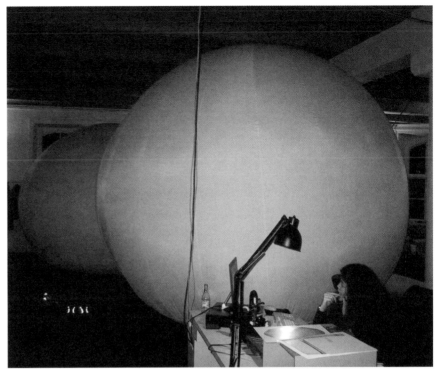

Early rendering of *Cloud*

Monica Förster's exhibition architecture arrives at the Snowcrash office

A scale model of *Cloud*

CLOUD, 2002

The first copy of Monica Förster's *Cloud* arrived at the Snowcrash office the very same morning that everyone was leaving to catch the flight for the show in Milan. *Cloud* went on to be listed as one of the best new inventions in 2004 by Time Magazine, and approximately 70 units of *Cloud* were produced by Snowcrash in Sweden in 2002-2003.

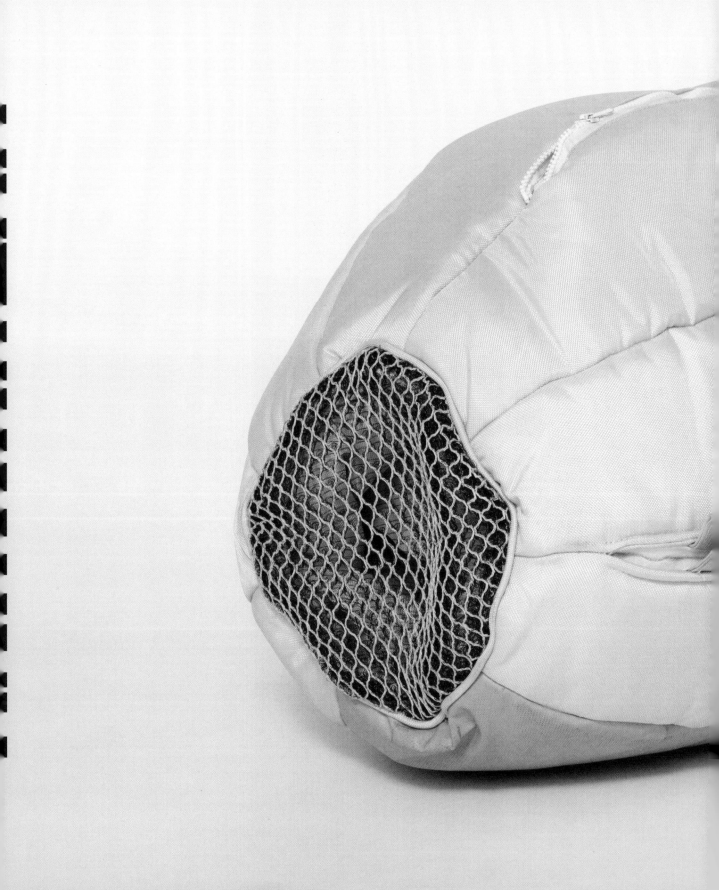

8. Lydholm, Eva-Lott. Stockholm 2018. Interview May 21st.
9. 2002. Spray VD blir utvecklare hos Robert Weil [CEO at Spray becomes developer for Robert Weil]. *Dagens Industri*. April 17th, 55.
10. Almqvist, Casten. Stockholm 2018. Interview April 20th.

customers what Snowcrash was about, but had felt the lack of output on the production side.

'The *Soundvawe* panels, *Globlow* and *Airbag* were the big sellers and we sold particularly well in Japan. It was easy to sell Snowcrash to high end design stores and agents with a special interest in design, but for them in turn to sell to their customers seemed hard. We said that it was design for the new work environment, and many knew us since we received so much press, but one problem was that we did not get any new products to sell. And then there was a constant change in management, and when Casten Almqvist started, everybody felt that we had reached a point where we had to turn things around or close down.'[8]

Proventus was aware of the problems, and recognised that they had reached a pivotal point where they needed to make an assessment of the venture, to see how it could be turned around financially. So, shortly after the successful launch of *Cloud*, Casten Almqvist was hired to share the title of CEO with Pio Barone Lumaga at Art & Technology by Proventus. Casten Almqvist came from the world of advertising and had become known in the Swedish press as 'Casten med kvasten' (Casten the cleaner) after having thoroughly negotiated cut downs, resignations and finally the closure of the failing IT company Spray, where he had served as vice CEO. Casten Almqvist's official mission at Snowcrash was to look for new acquisitions that could join under the Proventus umbrella; oversee international sales; and handle the expansion of the current companies.[9] But there would be no time to look for new acquisitions.

'For me Snowcrash was a joyride. I joined a company that was a success in several ways, one being its ability to attract top talent. I had the honour of working together with some very talented people at Snowcrash. My first conclusion was that Snowcrash was stuck in the middle as a business project; as if it had not been decided whether it was to be a straight forward commercial company or more of a philanthropic enterprise. Was it an art project or a business idea? Consequently the company lacked fundamental direction. It was completely experimental which in itself was fascinating and fun to be part of. However, it was also making a heavy loss and simply not sustainable. It took me about half a year to realise that it was not possible to save the company, at least not without investing massively at high risk. That wasn't an option since our owner already had put substantial amounts of money into the Snowcrash adventure. We should all be thankful that Robert had the vision and guts to give it a try. It was beautiful all the way to the end.'[10]

While the financial projections were being worked out and it soon became clear that the company was not going to make it, the design process nonetheless continued with high intensity in the belief that a new and commercial product could help the situation. In 2001, Arik Levy had designed *Getset*, an adaptable work desk with multiple stor-

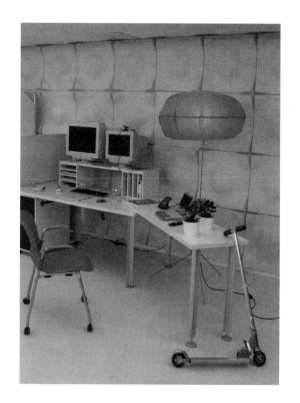

Trying out the flexible *Getset* module system at the Snowcrash office in 2001

GETSET, 2001

'*Getset* was based on a rather simple manufacturing technique that offered a lot of flexibility. It was a personal office that you could modify and expand based on the accessories that you accumulate over time. It was also an answer to the type of companies that emerged during the IT-boom, the tech start-ups, that needed to set up a high quality office landscape quickly and easily. The idea behind this system was to make it sociologically, culturally and economically viable. The product would come on a pallette and in something like ten minutes you would be ready, like speedy boarding with an airline. Our system would allow companies to set up an office faster than with any other office system. This would of course save them money for the rent of the space, so we also had plans to establish connections with the real estate world.' -Arik Levy

11. Tromp, Jan. 2020. Telephone interview April 24th.
12. Andersson, Hans och Svensson, Johan. Stockholm 2020. Interview February 18th.
13. Lumaga Barone, Pio. 2018. Skype interview September 29th.

age modules—and it had long been felt at Snowcrash that a task chair was missing to put in front of it. Ever since Herman Miller had released the *Aeron* chair (1992) designed by Bill Stumpf and Don Chadwick, it had become the task chair that others measured by—even though few had the muscles to develop a competitor. Snowcrash's answer to this was designed by the architect Jan Tromp from Valvomo.

'The starting point for me was to try and get as far away from the conventional image of a task chair as possible, so instead of something mechanical and stylish, I tried to make it familiar to the user. I came to think of the taxi drivers in warmer climates who use these plaids with wooden beads to cover their seats; it struck me as both an ergonomic and super non-stylish approach. If we made it well, the chair could express a kind of humble beginnings, something ordinary and still be a high-performing and technical task chair.'[11]

'We felt that there was a lot riding on this chair so we badly wanted it to meet the deadline. In order to have it ready in time for our presentation, we managed to convince the person from the Swedish test institute to test and approve the chair on December 24th, basically at the same time as that person was wrapping Christmas gifts. We made it, and after a presentation where we showed how it met all targets, we were expecting applauds, but the atmosphere in the meeting room was lukewarm and we closed down only days later.'[12]

The task chair *Taksi* by Jan Tromp had been delivered on time; Ulrika Mårtenssons collection of new sound absorbing textiles were ready to be launched; and the immense success in the press with Monica Förster's *Cloud;* along with many other projects that were being worked on, was not enough—the creativity was inferior to the larger structural problems and financial reality.

'I had the opportunity to work with great people, external designers, and we streamlined a shared design process, setting prototyping goals and quality control gateways. We re-defined beauty in an idiosyncratic way as the sum total of the qualities, while focusing on products that challenged common sense and yet appealed to the senses of the many. We started to build a commercial backbone offering products such as inflatable lights, a surfing chaise longue, sound proof tiles and more. We re-engineered an inflatable meeting space, the *Cloud*, worked on a new office chair concept, 'the taxi chair' and developed R&D for original products. There was a wonderful working atmosphere in Snowcrash, and it was fun to enhance the creativity of the collaborators. I enjoyed being in the background, cross fertilising ideas with people from different cultures, and pushing the design process to its limits. My experience is that great products emerge from a slow-cooking process. We were developing a line-up of new products that redefined customer experience and wellbeing, but after two years we clashed with the epitome of our time that required quick results.'[13]

On the 28th of January 2003, *Dagens Industri* reported that the operations of Snowcrash were put 'on ice', and that product devel-

TAKSI CHAIR - Jan Tromp, 2002

14. Huldschiner, Henrik. 2003. Casten Almqvist lägger ned Weil-bolag [Casten Almqvist closes down Weil company]. *Dagens Industri*. January 28th, 8.
15. Kvint, Annika. 2003. Svensk design förlorar spjutspets [Swedish Design loses its edge]. Dagens Nyheter. March 26th, 4.
16. Weil, Robert. Stockholm 2020. Interview February 13th.

opment and day-to-day operations were shut down, with existing customers to be served until the stock ran out.[14] In an article with the title 'Swedish design loses its edge', published two months later in Sweden's biggest newspaper *Dagens Nyheter*, design critic Annika Kvint wrote about the loss of 'Swedens most experimental design company'.[15] Despite financial security from Proventus and Robert Weil's genuine belief in the company, harnessing the creativity and putting it in a machinery had proven harder than anyone involved in Snowcrash could have ever imagined.

'This ownership occurred during an exceptional period in time, the 'dot.com era', when the old clashed with the new. Let us say that the car industry, to use an example, was not the first to adapt to internet. The old industry and industrialists looked at this event with great scepticism, and this stood in stark contrast to new parties who ran fast and only saw possibilities with this technology. What was happening in terms of creativity was absolutely right, but it was detached from the financial reality—many of the young tech companies that started simply lacked the experience and did not live in relation to the established industrial world. Proventus speculated against this bubble on the stock market, but we still believed in and wanted to embrace what was happening. We wanted Snowcrash to be young, live its own life, and have a drive to experiment. Therefore we gave total freedom for the creative process, so we later could merge that with our knowledge about production and distribution and turn it into an industrial company that could compete with the major international design brands.

'Given our background, I believe Proventus was the perfect owner for Snowcrash. We brought in people from different creative fields to create a mix that could pair the arts with industry—something which I have always believed to be crucial. This was however still not enough if we look at the result, because it turned out that Proventus also had problems with connecting the new with the old. But we can also acknowledge that all those companies that started during that era, Snowcrash included, were some twenty years too early.

'Maybe we were a bit naïve in all of this and gave too much freedom, but again, this is a very special time that we are talking about. Everything was changing and adapting to new technology, the workplace in particular. Snowcrash responded to this and the designers started to address issues such as sound and air. Some of the products were obviously too experimental, but that is where we stood—we were definitely outside the so called norm, but there is no doubt that what we produced was valid and 100% concrete.'[16]

Could it have survived if you had given it more time?

'A lot of what happened in Snowcrash was in the spirit of that time. The technology that was born then, exists today, and the industry eventually adapted to it. But at the time, it was a step into something unknown which everybody, old and new, had difficulty

17. Weil, Robert. Stockholm 2020. Interview February 13th.

dealing with. So, if we had taken it more slowly, maybe it would not have been so easy either. If I look in the mirror, sure, we could have done things a bit differently, but we could not have changed the time in which we worked.

'When we started to build Snowcrash the company, I did not want to set any restrictions. I did not want to start off by saying "we cannot do this and that because it costs too much". That would have inhibited the creativity and I believe many of the innovations we created would not have been made. But on the other hand, I have always had an immense respect for money—and I believe everybody involved also felt this. Maybe we expanded too fast, at a time when for example IT consultants could get almost any salary they wanted because they were in such high demand. So at one point I felt the need to put a limit on our investment. This limit was set at 100 million Swedish crowns. I believe we closed at around 110 million, but we also discussed the possibility of trying to reconstruct Snowcrash into a consulting company, since we had accumulated so much knowledge. But it was just not possible—it would have been too large an endeavour. I have always believed that failures are part of experimenting, key to learning and important for the process. Failure is one of the driving forces of development. You need to give space to failure; something good always comes out of it'.[17]

Like sightings of white elk, design patrons are rare in Sweden, and this is as true today as it was twenty years ago. That an investment company, almost exclusively operating in the world of banking, would invest 110 million SEK to turn a small design exhibition by a group of twenty-something designers with shaggy hair, into a design company without any demand on the creative output, could almost be called a freak accident. But a scenario where someone by accident would deposit that amount onto the wrong bank account on a Sunday morning is not comparable, because it is obvious that it was not sheer money that made a difference in this case—it was the faith of a true patron of the arts. It was a person who did not need, but felt the need to, invest and put faith in what creative people can accomplish when given the plattform to do what they do best. And the outcome is as you have just read in this book—undeniable innovations—which will be further examined and put into context in the following chapter.

GLOBLOW - Vesa Hinkola, Markus Nevalainen, Rane Vaskivuori, 1996

LIGHT PUNCH, 2000

Snowcrash focussed on people's wellbeing in the office and themes such as 'exercising at work' were discussed. Markus Nevalainen proposed a lamp that you could interact with in various ways to encourage movement. Hitting, swinging or pushing the lamp turns it on. Held in a diagonal position, it will dim until the desired level of light is reached, and the lamp is returned back to a vertical position. To turn the light off, you embrace it.

GLOBLOW FLOOR LAMP 02 - Vesa Hinkola, Markus Nevalainen, Rane Vaskivuori, 1996

GLOBLOW POLE - Vesa Hinkola, Markus Nevalainen, Rane Vaskivuori, 2002

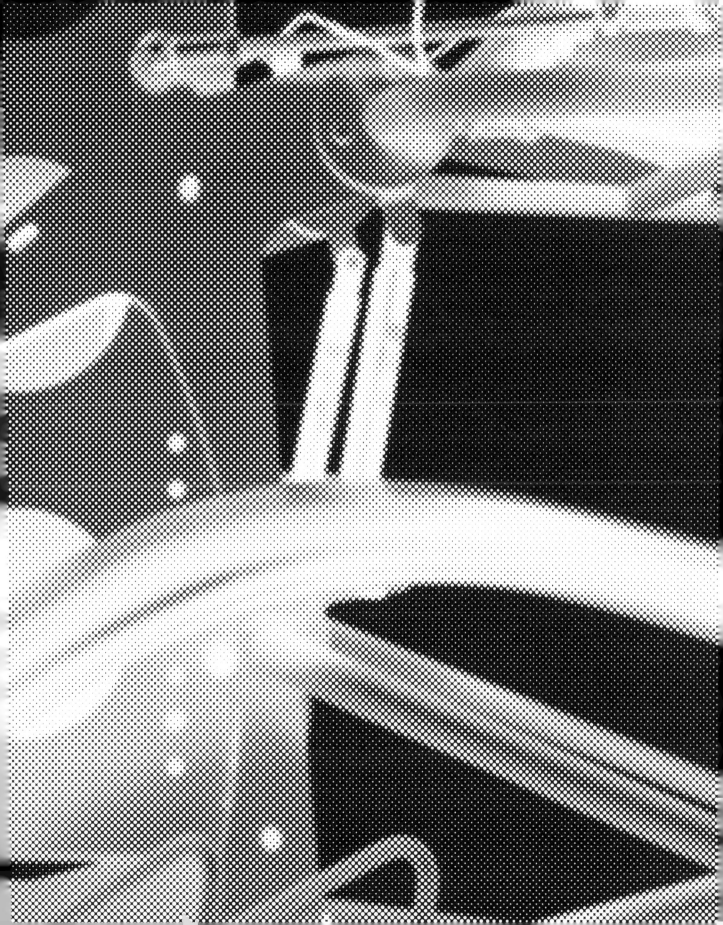

LOOKING FORWARD

1. Petruchi, Amanda. 2020. Kim Gordon is home again. *The New Yorker.* April 30th. https://www.newyorker.com/culture/the-new-yorker-interview/kim-gordon-on-instagram-ambition-and-los-angeles?fbclid=IwAR1kVGb8FuyyzzK5gK0Qwn-IGUM_kCTcbVFISYLODBoxb6KFSPFbX8-Sf6g (2020-05-03)
2. Stritzler-Levine, Widman, Dag and Winter, Karin. 2006. *Bruno Mathsson*. Bokförlaget Arena, 87.

Looking back at the period from the Snowcrash exhibition in 1997 to 2003 when the company was put on ice, and the conversation that it generated among visitors to their exhibitions and in the press, it is easy to see how it evolved into a folk tale within the design community. This is a scenario that happens when there is no clear recollection of what happened, and no source to go to for a coherent review—probably the same fate could not be achieved today, when we share all our memories online. But when asking about Snowcrash, most people remember that it had to do with technology.

When the American artist Kim Gordon commented on social media in an interview for *The New Yorker*, she said '…social media, the internet—I mean, there's no going back. Using it for ways it maybe wasn't intended is good. But what intentions does it have? It's only the people behind it. Technology is like nature—innocent'.[1] As Kim Gordon puts it, the technology is there and how it is used is up to each and every person—meaning that it can evolve in any direction. The designers connected to Snowcrash all had different ideas about how technology would progress, and this is reflected in the various objects in the collection.

Netsurfer was designed to accommodate the technology at hand and materialises a first encounter with IT, and the long hours of befriending it. *Netsurfer* offers a generous space for a fat monitor and tower computer case, and the overall layout of the piece is derived from the familiar image of a person riding a motorcycle. You sit with your legs apart in order to come closer to the centre—the engine. *Netsurfer* offers the sensation of feeling that your whole body has become one with the computer, because you cannot physically turn away from it, you are locked in. To go to an extreme, it is like the Japanese artist Atsuko Tanaka (1932–2005) putting on her *Electric Dress* in 1956—surrounded by lamps connected by electric cords, it detached her from reality and made her become one with the emergence of a society dependent on electronics.

When *Netsurfer* was introduced to the market it joined other proposals for how to work with computers: they could be hidden in cupboards to camouflage them at home; or used on different fixed or mobile workstations at the office. But designs that featured a reclined seat in combination with a computer such as in *Netsurfer,* were rare—one notable example that later followed was the *Surf Chair* (2000) by Danish design duo Kenneth Lylover & Leif Sørensen.

An early example of sitting in a reclined position in a composition of seat and desk for the work at hand—be it writing a letter, reading a book or typing on a machine—can be found in the oeuvre of the Swedish furniture designer Bruno Mathsson (1907–1988). Already in his debut exhibition at Röhsska museet in Gothenburg in 1936, he exhibited resting chairs complemented by height-adjustable reading tables.[2] And in 1941 you could read the following conversation with Bruno Mathsson in a local newspaper:

180–181
Netsurfer close up

Bruno Mathsson's Vilstol nr 36 with detachable book stand, 1936

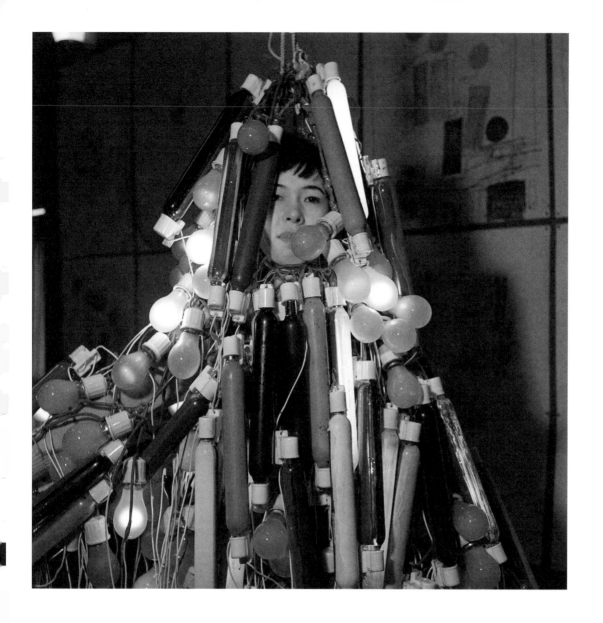

Atsuko Tanaka, *Electric Dress*,
taken at the 2nd Gutai Art
Exhibition, 1956

3. Stritzler-Levine, Widman, Dag and Winter, Karin. 2006. *Bruno Mathsson*. Bokförlaget Arena, 87.
4. Åkerblom, Bengt. 1948. Standing and sitting posture: with special reference to the construction of chairs, Kungl. Karolinska Institutet, Norstedt, 183.
5. Dunne, Anthony. 2005. *Hertzian Tales–electronic Products, Aesthetic Experiences and Critical Design*. MIT Press, 17–19.
6. Dunne, Anthony. 2005. *Hertzian Tales – Electronic Products, Aesthetic Experiences and Critical Design*. MIT Press, 43, 67.

Cluvens' *Scorpion Computer Cockpit*, 2020

'Bruno Mathsson: This for example, is a chair for work. Interviewer: But surely you cannot half lay down and work! Bruno Mathsson: But sure you can. I handle all my correspondence in a chair of this kind, half laying down with the machine in my lap. Who has said, that the machine should stand on a table and that you yourself have to sit and become tired in the lumbar region…'[3]

This attitude differed from the general view on a correct ergonomic position for work at that time, which was more in line with the research by Swedish doctor Bengt Åkerblom (1901–1990). In his dissertation in 1948, *Standing and sitting posture—with special reference to the construction of chairs*, he declared that a reclined seat formed after the body did not give enough support for the lumbar region, and that the best way was to have a seat which enabled different postures.[4] Recommendations such as these have however been neglected by the many people who work from home today—horizontally thrown on their sofas with a phone or laptop. And in this sense—with its reclined seat—*Netsurfer* can still claim to be highly functional for its purpose. When put in the context of the gaming industry, it can be regarded as an archetype, and is not only still highly functional but also aesthetically not too deviant, as becomes evident when looking at recent models like the *Scorpion Computer Cockpit* by Cluvens (2020).

One of the problems with design that supports electronic hardware or has integrated electronics, is that the design itself runs the risk of becoming obsolete since technology constantly evolves. But as the example of *Netsurfer* shows, these designs do not necessarily become obsolete by default, as is also argued in the book *Herzian Tales–Electronic Products, Aesthetic Experience, and Critical Design*. Its author Anthony Dunne suggests that in a juxtaposition of material and electronic culture, each element is developed in relation to its own aesthetic and functional potential: 'No effort need be made to reconcile the different scales of the electronic and the material. They can simply coexist in one object. …Cultural obsolescence need not occur at the same rate as technological obsolescence'.[5]

The TV cabinet/table *Jack in the box* and lamp *Globlow* have integrated electronics and run the same risk of being obsolete as *Netsurfer*. But just like *Netsurfer,* both still function today and could by Anthony Dunne be defined with the term 'para-functionality' meaning 'a form of design where function is used to encourage reflection on how electronic products condition our behaviour. The prefix "para-" suggests that such design is within the realms of utility but attempts to go beyond conventional definitions of functionalism to include the poetic'.[6] *Jack in the box* does exactly what it is supposed to do—hold a TV in front of us to watch—but also offers the possibility to actively hide it, urging us to reflect on our addiction to it. *Globlow* lets the user experience how the lampshade is constructed every time it is turned on and off, visualising the lamp's condition beyond its basic function of producing light, and giving the user a deeper understanding of

7. Cremascoli, Olivia. 1996. Dove va l'ufficio? A casa. *Interni*. March issue, 109.
8. Saval, Nikil. 2014. *Cubed – A Secret History of the Workplace.* Doubleday, 201–205.

the object. The same effect can also be found in a contemporary to *Globlow* that was presented at the graduation show at Beckmans College of Design in 1996. Here, Swedish designer Eva Lilja Löwenhielm showed a series of floor lamps sewn in sail cloth, in which a light-switch activated a fan that inflated the lamp-shades.

Globlow LED took things one step further when it not only integrated electronic hardware but also software. It presents the idea that you can interact with the product wirelessly and at a distance. It echoes Nikola Tesla's first attempts to wirelessly light a Geissler tube in the late 19th century; and also *The Clapper,* launched in the 1980s by Joseph Enterprises, which allowed you to turn your light on and off by clapping your hands. Even though few understood the point of being able to use your mobile phone to turn on and off, and change the colour of the light in *Globlow LED* in 2000, it nearly constitutes an oracle, since today we control almost all appliances with our phones. *Infinite lamp* draws things to a full circle by becoming a response to the very thing that *Jack in the box* strives to resist. When there is no other source of light, *Infinite lamp* shines through the screen and lays bare our total dependence on technology.

The Snowcrash collection embodies different concepts, with some objects meant as 'one-offs' and others for mass production. Although most of these designs never actually reached a market, the outspoken ambition of the company was to develop this collection towards the office environment, where there was an opportunity to sell because there was a need and a desire for new typologies and aesthetics.

The movie *Ghostbusters* (1984) proved that ghosts exist, but when one of its main characters, Dr Egon Spengler, proclaimed that 'print is dead!', it simply wasn't true—the paperless society that was expected as a result of computers entering our lives in the 1980s, still has not happened. The coming of the paperless workspace underlines that it is hard to predict what will become the norm when facing new technology. It might be difficult to understand that you could know so little about what we take for granted today, but as has been discussed in previous chapters, nobody knew where IT would take us. There was an overall uncertainty in the furniture industry in how to respond to this development in the 1990s, as shown by an editorial in the 1996 March issue of Italian magazine *Interni*: 'Some say that at the latest presentations in Milan of office furnishings there were few surprises because, apart from the lasting slump in demand which has slowed production investment, the manufacturers have become more cautious because of the uncertainty of the evolution of the very concept of work, its organisation and, above all, about where to do it'.[7]

The office that adapted to the IT society in the 1990s was built on the idea of the *Bürolandschaft* (Office landscape) that had taken root in Germany in the late 1950s[8], and which had evolved over the decades. The driving forces behind the evolution of the office are

9. Herman Miller. Action Office System. https://www.hermanmiller.com/products/workspaces/workstations/action-office-system/design-story/ (2020-05-10)
10. Saval, Nikil. 2014. *Cubed – A Secret History of the Workplace*. Doubleday, 202.
11. Fahraeus, Leila. 1969. Facit och kontorslandskapet, *Möbelvärlden*. Nr3, 54.
12. Gordan, Dan. 2002. *Svenska stolar*. Byggförlaget, 215.
13. Björkman, Helena; Dymling, Claes. 1988. *Ralph Erskine, arkitekt*. Byggförlaget, 110, 128, 213.
14. Rönn, Magnus. 2000. *Ralph Erskine som industriarkitekt*. Svensk Byggtjänst, 143.

Herman Miller's *Action Office*

The office interior of Pågens Bakery, Malmö, 1969

related to architecture, technology, the economy and social changes. And in the 1960s, the times they were a-changin'. After decades of war, individual liberation was claimed in force and the office became more focused towards individual needs. Walls came down and desks were reshuffled to increase effectivity. Development of furniture is fundamental to changing the layout in the office, and the introduction of the *Action Office* in 1964 and 1968, developed at the American furniture company Herman Miller, was credited with being 'the world's first open-plan office system'. It consisted of 'a set of components that could be combined and recombined to become whatever an office needed to be over time'.[9]

Sweden was an early adopter of the office landscape[10] and in 1969 the office furniture system *Facit 80* (1969) designed by Swede Carl Christiansson (1932–2017) was presented at the furniture fair Kontor-Data in Stockholm. It was hailed in the Swedish press as a radical new solution and one magazine wrote: 'Quick communication, decision making and the possibility for teamwork are the advantages of an office landscape ...this system means, in a way, a democratising of the office'.[11] *Facit 80* addressed layout, air, sound, light, and included a task chair, mobile storage unit, console table, telephone desk, mobile planter and freestanding screens in strong colours. The producer, Facit, was a Swedish company that developed and manufactured calculators and typewriters, and when its furniture division introduced *Facit 80*, nothing compared to it in Scandinavia. Having been measured after the international paper size format it also did well abroad and was favoured by companies such as IBM.[12]

The office interior of the bakery Pågens (1969) in Malmö, by British/Swedish architect Ralph Erskine, was a timely representation of the ideas of an office landscape. Here, windows on all sides allowed natural light to enter the room, and wall surfaces were covered with wooden laths to improve acoustics. The individual desks that were designed for the office offered privacy as well as the opportunity to communicate with colleagues, and electric cables were drawn into the legs of the desks from outlets in the floor.[13] The following notes by Ralph Erskine explain his thoughts behind the concept, which he called *Antianonymous*:

'Motto: Work is for and, a part of, people. People don't exist for work.' No symbols of hierarchy, leader, status... it is in team psychological situations very debatable, that a boss is the only one with his own room!!! Better if he sits "with the gang" and meets his need... neither house or tables solves problems obviously, but hopefully they can help, help!!'[14]

The introduction of new management styles and smarter, cheaper and smaller work tools in the 1990s, meant that work did not have to be done at the desk. This made the layout of the office landscape more fluid than before, and the 'in-between' work spaces where people socialised came into focus. The increase of small talk and noisy digital

15. Troxler, Rina. 2019. Email February 21st.
16. Almaas Helsing, Ingerid. 2002. Divine Absurdity. *Frame*. Sep/Oct issue, 110.

Interior of Der Spiegel Publishing house, Hamburg, 1969

gadgets in this environment highlighted the need for good acoustics. This aspect was addressed with *The Sound Solution Collection* and the *Soundwave* panels. The *Soundwave* panels were designed to efficiently break soundwaves and give a harmonious expression when multiplied, and can today be regarded as one of the earliest examples of an industrialised wall mounted acoustic panel. A blueprint for such a product can be found in 1969 in the interior designed by Verner Panton (1926–1998) for the new headquarters of the newspaper *Der Spiegel* in Hamburg. Architect Rina Troxler, who worked closely with Verner Panton, explains its origin like this: 'With the hard stone floors and large glass windows, the acoustics in the building were poor, and in a highly political atmosphere such as a publishing house, secrecy was paramount, so Panton developed a geometrically shaped acoustic panel in various depths to mount on walls and ceilings'.[15] The importance of this kind of solution increased over the years, and by 2021 the variations of acoustic products on the market are seemingly endless.

The free flow of interaction in the office landscape also triggered a need for secluded areas in which to have a private conversation or a mental break. This was typically solved by shielding yourself off with screens in various formats, or hiding in furniture with high backrests, and for this reason Snowcrash developed a series of space dividers named *Slip*. *Cloud* provides the same answer in a larger format. It is a room within the room, and with its semi-transparent ripstop nylon, it creates a personal space that shields you from outside distraction. In 2002, the same year that *Cloud* was launched, a variation on this idea could be found in the interior of the ad agency Dante in Oslo, created by Norwegian MMW Architects. Here, pneumatic structures created rooms made out of a '…woven PVC material developed in collaboration with clothing manufacturer Helly Hansen, which was similar to the fireproof fabric used to make survival kits for companies working in the North Sea'.[16] These kinds of solutions did not however become a common sight at offices; instead the screens and high backrest furniture prevailed, and in recent years 'pods'—small soundproofed booths—have been placed in office landscapes to cater to the same needs.

The emergence of wireless communication in the 1990s expanded the realm of the office. It allowed people to work wherever they wanted to, be it at a café, in the park or on the street. This 'nomadic' work style was then, as now, limited to the quality of reception, battery time and optional aids such as furniture. Inflated, *Cloud* is big enough for several people, and in a deflated condition it fits in a bag that can be carried over your shoulder and used wherever you need it—as long as you can supply it with electricity. Used outside, it creates an ephemeral architecture for different activities that protects against the elements. Preceding *Cloud* in this manner are the so called 'inflatables' made in 1969 by a collective of architects based in San Francisco,

17. Dreyfus, Sylvia; Hurr, Doug; Kitrilakis, Sotiti; Lord, Chip; Marquez, Hudson; Nichels, Doug; Schreier, Curtis; Shapiro, Andy and Tilford, Charley. 1971. *Inflatocookbook*. Ant Farm, January, 2.
18. Dreyfus, Sylvia; Hurr, Doug; Kitrilakis, Sotiti; Lord, Chip; Marquez, Hudson; Nichels, Doug; Schreier, Curtis; Shapiro, Andy and Tilford, Charley. 1971. *Inflatocookbook*. Ant Farm, January, 7.
19. Final Home. About. https://www.finalhome.com/ABOUT (2020-05-10)

Interior of advertising agency Dante, Oslo, 2002

who called themselves Ant Farm. By using polyethylene, tape and fans, they 'built numerous demo-inflatables at schools, conferences, festivals and gatherings around the state of California and beyond'.[17] They produced an *Inflatocookbook* with instructions to show others how to build their own inflatable, and the different organically shaped designs carried names such as *Rainbow Orchard*, *Shining Sea* and *Dreamcloud*. Although there is no connection to Ant Farm's outspoken anti-consumerism and thoughts on the mass-media in the late 1960s, the aesthetic and their idea of a mobile temporary room for various activities resonates with *Cloud*. As it is explained in their *Inflatocookbook*: 'The new-dimensional space becomes more or less whatever people decide it is—a temple, a funhouse, a suffocation torture-device, a pleasure dome. A conference party, wedding, meeting, regular Saturday afternoon becomes a festival'.[18]

A concentrated version of using a mobile product to support and protect your mind and body in an urban environment, can be represented by the Japanese fashion designer Kosuke Tsumura's nylon coat *Final Home* (1994), produced by the company of the same name. With 28 or 44 pockets, it is 'clothing which can be adapted according to need. To protect against the cold, you can put newspapers in the pockets, or if you equip it with survival rations and a medical kit, it becomes a valuable piece of clothing when taking refuge'. It equates to the idea of being the 'ultimate shelter'[19] and also supports another kind of nomadism, that of necessity—aiding people displaced as a result of conflicts or catastrophes. After the Covid-19 outbreak in 2020, new measures had to be taken into account to prevent the disease from spreading. Past and present solutions for a mobile room that shields you are more relevant than ever to consider—and now they

Kosuke Tsumura in a prototype of the *Final Home* nylon coat, taken in midwinter in Kabukicho, Shinjuku, Tokyo, 1992

20. Block, India. 2020. Sun Dayong designs wearable shield to protect against coronavirus outbreaks. *Dezeen*. https://www.dezeen.com/2020/02/26/sun-dayong-coronavirus-protection-shield/?li_source=LI&li_medium=rhs_block_2 (2020-02-30)

should also guarantee social distancing. Perhaps as it has been envisioned by Chinese architect Sun Dayong in his *Be a Bat Man* (2020), a design that offers a 'unique, private mobile space for people'.[20]

There are several objects in the Snowcrash collection that in different ways address or directly support the idea of a nomadic work- and life-style. The bags *Addapt* and *Loco* are, as it was marketed, 'portable work pads' designed for a modern way of life where people do not have to choose, featuring clip on bags and multiple pockets to fit other daily essentials beyond the compulsory laptop. *Airbag* and *Nomad Chair* are evidently designed to serve someone on the move, as they are flexible and easy to bring along. Both are perfectly contemporary, but also strongly linked to the past. *Airbag*'s aesthetic and functionality connects it to the radical Italian design of the 1960s–80s, but without the irony. The enlarged cushion, which constitute the entire furniture, is a play with scale. Further, the fact that you can attach multiple *Airbags* with its straps—so people can share one big mattress—gives it social relevance. The economical and transparent solutions of the *Nomad Chair*, and its temporary nature, make it a reincarnation of the Italian designer Lina Bo Bardi's *Roadside chair* (1967). It continues the probing of the vernacular, but in a modern setting, since it is a direct result of the living conditions, culture and values found in a dense urban area. The *Nomad Chair* also sits close to the portable collapsible chair, and the very identity of this typology is what the *Zikzak* chair tries to manipulate, exploring if it is considered to be more or less of a chair by being designed with a heavy and intricate mechanism instead of a simple lightweight construction.

Lina Bo Bardi on the *Roadside chair*, c. 1967

21. Golling, Daniel; Kjellin, Gustaf. 2018. *Helt vildt! – The Second Golden Age of Danish Design*. Summit, 77.
22. Wagner, Monika. 2015. Materiality. *Material*. Whitechapel Gallery, 26.

One approach that connects to all of these seats with their individual qualities, is that of *Stool Pants* (2002) by the Dutch designer Richard Hutten for Japanese producer E&Y. Although it can be argued that it is not practical at all times, it rises to the challenge of offering the optimal design for a portable and comfortable seat—by letting you wear the furniture as a pair of pants.

After Snowcrash was put on ice in 2003 and the IT bubble had burst, it seemed that people's thirst for the new and unknown had subsided and a craving for something comprehensible and familiar, such as handicraft, took hold. Many producers now turned their attention to the innovation of the business of design—rather than design. At the end of the 2000s, we started to enjoy 3G, the third generation of mobile networks, and 'apps' became as popular as websites had been in the 1990s. In this decade several young furniture companies such as the Danish producers HAY (2002) and Muuto (2006) emerged. Enabled by globalization, they successfully combined outsourced production with talented designers to create price-worthy collections ranging from accessories to modular sofas. In the 2010s, 4G allowed us to share more things online, and the image based culture that it created was the battle ground for the companies that offered 'affordable design'. This progressed in tandem with the domestication of the office landscape, as Kristian Byrge, the CEO of Muuto described it in the book *Helt Vildt—The Second Golden Age of Danish Design*: 'There is a trend towards the office getting more "homey", and this has suited us well. Before, everything was either black or white, but now you want things more pleasant, and it's okay to have more colours and wood, and it's preferable it be products that you can relate to in a private context …the break out areas—the pantry, the canteen, the informal meeting rooms, the areas that give identity and a mood to the office—that is where we are a good match'.[21]

The ideal office gradually turned into a single shared living room, offered by the hour at co-working spaces. Investments in experiments and product development slowed down as an effect of the fierce competition on price—and the closeness to the consumers on social media dictated the aesthetics—resulting in an increasingly predictable output of generic design. This development was felt on both sides of the Atlantic, which became evident when Knoll acquired Muuto in 2017 and Herman Miller acquired HAY, in 2019.

One main feature that defines the design language of Snowcrash, is the use of unconventional materials to achieve new expressions and functionality. The German art historian Monika Wagner wrote: 'The substances and objects that constitute material are subject to transformation through processing, and hence they reveal information about the forces of production at the time or a historical technique'.[22] There is no apparent information that reveals a particular force of production or historical technique that connects the collection to a

23. Snowcrash. 1999. *Snowcrash Materialised Home*. Proventus Design. Press release April. https://www.scandinaviandesign.com/snowcrash/press.html (2018-05-03)
24. Meindertsma, Christien. Flax Chair 2015. https://christien-meindertsma.com/Flax-Chair (2020-04-10)

specific time—such as voluptuous furniture moulded in plastic that can be tied to the 1960s. Snowcrash sampled a wide variety of materials produced in various techniques—but one thing that is notable is their frequent use of synthetic materials instead of natural, and this inspiration came primarily from the fashion and sports industry. Different kinds of nylon were used, as well as composite materials common in transport and outdoor activities for their durability and practicality. This gives the collection a look and tactility that triggers curiosity instead of communicating exclusivity or a value, like the use of brass, leather or hardwood does. As stated in the press release for their exhibition in Milan in 1999, 'steel, rubber, polymer fibres, polythene and polystyrene are examples of materials responsible for many innovations in product design. With synthetic materials, it is possible to create light and transparent design and add sensual features to products. New materials are profitable to produce. Synthetic materials can also be long-lasting, but still ecological'.[23]

The use of sustainable materials was a topic at Snowcrash and many of the synthetic materials showed promise, but there was no clear strategy worked out for it in production. Since the 2000s, the focus on recyclable materials has increased and an holistic approach to sustainability has 'almost' become common practice in the design industry. Today, there are a large number of designers and producers who actively put resources into developing furniture in new experimental, environmentally friendly materials and production methods. One example is the Dutch designer Christien Meindertsma with her biodegradable *Flax Chair* (2015), which made use of the natural material flax in combination with a biodegradable textile, moulded into a rigid chair[24]—an innovation that has influenced other companies to industrialise the process.

In 2018 Sheila Hicks' exhibition *Migdalor* opened at Magasin III's satellite space in Jaffa. Here, a selection of Hicks's sculptural fibre-art installations were shown, among them the monumental *Saffron Sentinel* (2017), composed of 200 large bales made out of fibres in strong colours. Visitors could experience what Sheila Hicks has manifested in many of her works over the years—how fibres can be in dialogue with architecture. This way of thinking about, and working with fibre, seems to have been the ambition of many of the designers at Snowcrash, since a large part of the Snowcrash collection is fibre driven. Natural or enhanced fibres are used in ways that go beyond the mere practical to add an additional layer to the object, so it reaches new resonance in a space.

Fibres have also been worked with to give a traditional product new properties. Experiments with a wide variety of fibres and variations of woven structures resulted in *The Sound Solution Collection*, a series of textiles with sound absorbing qualities. This approach is similar to that of the development of textiles made with glass fibres in the past. The method of producing glass fibre was industrialised in

Installation view of Sheila Hicks' *Saffron Sentinel* (2017) at the exhibition *Migdalor*, Magasin III in Jaffa, 2018

25. Hald, Arthur. 1946. Vardagstyg i vardande. Fakta om glastyget – intervju med Astrid Sampe-Hultberg. *Form*. Issue 2, 23.
26. Hald, Arthur. 1946. Vardagstyg i vardande. Fakta om glastyget – intervju med Astrid Sampe-Hultberg. *Form*. Issue 2, 22.
27. Von Platen, Jenny. 2016. Viola Gråsten. Björnberg, Julia; Wickman, Kerstin; Widenheim, Cecilia (editors). *Oomph – The Women who Made Sweden Colorful*. Malmö Konstmuseum, 99.
28. Hård Af Segerstad, Ulf. 1963. Det dynamiska möbel-Finland [The dynamic furniture-Finland]. Svenska Dagbladet. October 4th, 17.
29. Advertisement. 1960. Edsbyverken – Scandinavia's largest manufacturer of chairs, tables, skis. Svenska Dagbladet. April 2nd, 27.
30. Arwidson, Bertil. 2006. *Från Snickeri till Möbelindustri – 100 år med Sveriges Möbelindustriförbund*. AB Svensk Byggtjänst, 100.
31. Jansson, Rolf. 2013. *Stil o. Kvalitet När Klaessons möblerade världen*. Lekerbergs Sparbank 138.

Astrid Sampe making a fire resistance test of a glass fibre textile at Nordiska Kompaniet textile chamber, in collaboration with Mölnlycke. Textile by Astrid Sampe

America at the same time as artificial fibres like Nylon, and typically used in products such as insulation tape, movie screens or sanitary products.²⁵ The Swedish textile designer Astrid Sampe (1909–2002) was among those who saw the potential in it, and in 1946 she developed and presented textiles such as drapes and upholstery fabric made with glass fibre. Astrid Sampe pushed for it to become commercialised since 'a fabric produced out of glass fibre has exceptional qualities—it does not burn, is not sensitive to light or affected by mildew or insects, and is easy to clean'.²⁶

Considering how Snowcrash originated and developed, it constitutes a rare but not unique merger of visionary ideas from Finland, and Swedish industrial know how—as the following examples show. The Finnish textile designer Viola Gråsten (1910–1994), who came to Sweden in 1944, 'attained a prominent position when it comes to bringing colour to Swedish homes'.²⁷ Working closely with companies such as NK Textiles (NK: Textilkammare) and later with Mölnlycke Weaving Company as its artistic director, Viola Gråsten designed a great deal of unconventional patterns and non-figurative motifs in what were at the time daring colour combinations. Patterns such as *Oomph* (1952) went on to become influential. She also developed products that became much loved classics, like the blanket *Snark* (Snore) in 1957 for Tidstrand's Wool Factory.

The Finnish architect and designer Ilmari Tapiovaara (1914–1999) was known in Sweden for his collaboration with the Finnish company ASKO—which in the 1960s was the largest furniture producer in Finland and Scandinavia.²⁸ The Swedish ski manufacturer Edsbyverken, which in the 1940s was trying to diversify its business and branch out into the furniture industry, engaged Tapiovaara, and in 1955 he successfully revamped their wooden chair *Fanett* and contributed to Edsbyverken's establishment as a furniture producer. He followed up with table *No.741*, chair *No.57*.²⁹ and the chair *No.59, Mademoiselle* (1958–59), which in the 1960s become a big seller with 10,000 units produced.³⁰

The Swedish furniture producer Klaessons was founded in 1886 and reached a prominent position after World War Two through several high profile interior projects with names such as Carl Malmsten, Peter Celsing and Astrid Sampe. At the end of the 1980s, the company needed to adapt to the market's need for new office furniture, and sought the help from Finnish design duo Yrjö Wiherheimo and Simo Heikkilä. Wiherheimo and Heikkilä's *Flok* series (1992)—which consisted of a stackable chair, armchair, easy chair and table—became a commercial success and found its way into universities, airports and hospitals in Sweden and abroad. Their successful collaboration was renewed in 1997 with the chair *Adam*, and together with *Flok* it constituted nearly 35% of Klaessons total sales during the 1990s.³¹

32. Sotamaa, Yrjö. 1997. Resolving Everyday Problems – From Aalto to Snowcrash. *Frame*. Issue 1, 66–67.
33. Irvine, James. 2002. *Mårten Claesson Eero Koivisto Ola Rune*. Mårten Claesson Eero Koivisto Ola Rune.

It could be said that Snowcrash continued in what Finnish professor of design innovation, Yrjö Sotamaa, described in an article as a typical Finnish design tradition, which is that of 'the idea of experimentation or "playing" with materials'.[32] Designs by Finnish originators are heavily represented in the collection, but the team of designers and developers at Snowcrash were a highly international mix. In terms of nationality, there was some confusion in the press as to where to place Snowcrash, and as a result the company was dubbed Swedish, Finnish, Nordic and Scandinavian with equal emphasis. However, besides having drawn on its place of origin in the exhibition of 1997, using a geographical position to benefit from national traits was never a marketing tool consciously used by the company to sell the collection. This stands somewhat in contrast to their Nordic contemporaries who also targeted the office environment: predominantly Swedish, they used the re-established interest in the label 'Scandinavian design' in the 1990s to market themselves.

In Snowcrash, besides the names of the designers, the objects themselves did not signal anything aesthetically significant about its origin; there were no cultural connections to a specific region by using known ornaments or traditional materials. This set them further apart from other producers and designers based in Sweden, whose output of furniture aesthetically often drew inspiration from functionalism in the 1930s–50s and favoured traditional natural materials. This design can be labelled 'new modernism', and could be described with a quote by the British designer James Irvine (1958–2013), commenting on the wooden easy chair *Omni* (2001) by Swedish architects Claesson Koivisto Rune for Swedish producer Swedese: 'They had managed to design a piece which synthesised modernity with the new. The chair is not wild at all, it is perfectly functional, and technically innovative. Above all it is superbly Scandinavian'.[33] The adventurous Snowcrash collection does not fit this description, but it could be argued that it has an equal claim to the label if considering the ideals behind modernism: an optimism for the future; the urge to build something better and different than what had been; and using new materials and technology.

Maybe Snowcrash can even gently brush with 'critical design' if we consider it as defined in the book *Design Noir: The Secret Life of Electronic Objects* by Anthony Ray & Fiona Raby, that it 'rejects how things are now as being the only possibility, it provides a critique of the prevailing situation through designs that embody alternative social, cultural, technical or economic values'. Even though this is argued with consumer products such as electronic appliances in mind, this speaks to Snowcrash in parts—a link which is strengthened when considering the following line: 'there is a place for a form of design that pushes the cultural and aesthetic potential and role of electronic products and services to its limits. Questions must be asked about what we actually need, about the way poetic moments can be inter-

Chair *Omni* by Claesson Koivisto Rune, 2001

34. Dunne, Anthony and Raby, Fiona. 2001. *Design Noir: The Secret Life of Electronic Objects*. Birkhäuser, 58.
35. 2006. Dj Krush – Practice Video Magazine Issue 3. Youtube December 30th. https://www.youtube.com/watch?v=9q4huyQA7Y4 (2020-06-01)
36. Suppanen, Ilkka. 2020. Telephone interview, June 1st.

twined with the everyday and not separated from it'.[34] There certainly was no deliberate critique behind the designs at Snowcrash, and the intention clearly was to make an industrial and commercial leap. But that the discussion about design and what it can be in relation to technology, was highly valued and pushed to the limits, is obvious. As a result, the diverse collection that was made over the years is a rare case that did not follow the common template, and it therefore seems fitting not to fold Snowcrash into a pre-defined label, but instead say that Snowcrash constitutes its own. As DJ Krush—the groundbreaking Japanese musician who composed the sampled based soundtrack for the fashion brand Final Home's 1998 Autumn–Winter season show—once said: 'if you want to assign a genre to my music, you can call it DJ Krush music'.[35]

The press described designs from Snowcrash as 'futuristic' without the use of the prefix 'retro'. And although the name Snowcrash was borrowed from an iconic work in the sci-fi genre, references to gibsonian cyperpunk aesthetics are (perhaps with one or two exceptions) nowhere to be found in the objects. The designers behind Snowcrash have managed to steer clear of these obvious and tempting tracks often used when the future is to be designed, and they have managed to do so because they never for a second gazed backwards. Occupied with dealing with the present and imagining the future, everybody behind Snowcrash seems to have been looking forward. The result is a collection with its own design language, which was perhaps too unusual to succeed in commercial terms at the time, but which has certainly proven to be a success in terms of innovative design. Objects in the collection have remained relevant—foreseeing user behaviour and needs in interior environments—achievements that could only have been made possible by having an optimistic view on technology and the future.

When Snowcrash was active, the future looked bright and full of possibilities. Being largely unknown meant that the designers could approach their tasks with an innocence that was to their advantage. In 2021, the future is on the contrary quite known—it does not look too bright, and technology has proven to not always be used with good intentions. Ilkka Suppanen today shares his time between his studios in Helsinki and Milan, where he also teaches a course in design at the Polytechnic University.

'Those studying to become a designer today have it tough, since there is so much to clean up after previous generations' negligence. They are more burdened by the reality than I was when I was studying, because there is a constant news-flow with mostly bad news and plenty of accessible research about our future. So my biggest challenge when I am teaching, is to make the students not forget about looking at the future with optimism, since I know it can also create great possibilities.'[36]

Compared to twenty years ago, there is technology available today that the founders of Snowcrash could not even dream would be so easy to access and use; there is a greater awareness about design in society; and collaborations are borderless. Once again we are facing a big shift in technology, with the fifth generation of mobile networks replacing the fourth. Its speed will unleash something that is unpredictable, and only people can decide how far, or where it will go—this is as certain as the snow that will continue to fall in Finland and Sweden.

INDEX
The Snowcrash collection

NETSURFER [150-151]
Computer divan
Design: Teppo Asikainen, Ilkka Terho, 1995
Materials: Steel structure with grey powder coating, pressed plywood seat, black leather upholstery
Dimensions: H98xW78xD161 cm
First shown at Habitare fair, Helsinki, 1995
First produced by Netsurfer Ltd.
Part of the Snowcrash Exhibition 1997

NETSURFER MAX [54-55]
Computer divan
Design: Teppo Asikainen, Ilkka Terho, 1996
Materials: Steel structure with grey powder coating, pressed plywood seat, black leather upholstery
First shown at Snowcrash exhibition in Milan, 1997
First produced by Netsurfer Ltd.

NETSURFER LIGHT
Computer divan
Design: Teppo Asikainen, Ilkka Terho, 1998
Materials: Steel structure with grey powder coating, pressed plywood seat, black leather upholstery
First produced by Netsurfer Ltd.

CHIP [36-37]
Rocker
Design: Teppo Asikainen, Ilkka Terho, 1996
Materials: Pressed plywood seat on polyurethane base
Dimensions: H37xW60xD140 cm
Weight: 6kg
First shown at Helsinki Design Museum, 1996
First produced by Netsurfer Ltd.
Part of the Snowcrash Exhibition 1997

NOMAD CHAIR [35]
Design: Ilkka Suppanen, 1994
Materials: Felt, Spring steel
Dimensions: H80xW60xD60 cm
First shown at Varde, Nordic Design Programme under the name Seat 1,2
Part of the Snowcrash Exhibition 1997
Later produced by Gallerie Maria Wettergren

FLYING CARPET [82-83]
Sofa
Design: Ilkka Suppanen, 1997
Materials: Felt, Spring steel
Dimensions: H93,5xW101xD99 cm
First shown at Snowcrash exhibition, Milan, 1997
Later produced by Cappellini

FROZEN FEATHER [62-63]
Pendant lamp
Design: Ilkka Suppanen, 1997
Materials: Feather down, glass plates, light fixture
Dimensions: H80xW80xD60 cm
First shown at Snowcrash exhibition, Milan, 1997

AV RACK [66]
Cabinet
Design: Ilkka Suppanen, 1997
Textile design with Paula Tuomi and Jarkko Kallio
Materials: Steel frame and plastic woven textile
Dimensions: H150xW70xD50 cm
First shown at Snowcrash exhibition, Milan, 1997
Later produced by Cappellini

AIRBAG [70-73]
Seating furniture
Design: Pasi Kolhonen, Ilkka Suppanen, 1996
Materials: 100% Nylon upholstery cover, reinforced fibreglass back supports, polyester straps, polystyrene filling
Dimensions: Chair H80xW85xD80 cm, Mattress H25xL155xW85 cm
Part of the Snowcrash Exhibition 1997
First made for Netsurfer Design Ltd.

PLUSMINUS [58]
Modular sofa
Design: Jan Tromp, Rane Vaskivuori, 1997
Materials: Plywood, stainless steel, upholstery
Dimensions: H73xW60xD102 cm (per module)
First shown at Snowcrash exhibition, Milan, 1997

TOMAHAWK [57]
Table
Design: Ilkka Terho, Jan Tromp, Markus Nevalainen, 1997
Materials: Rocket-shaped body of laser-cut steel. In-built light with dimmer. Laminated glass with titanium oxide blown graphics
Module dimensions: H70xW120xD230 cm
First shown at Snowcrash exhibition, Milan, 1997

JACK IN THE BOX [31]
Table/Cabinet
Design: Timo Salli, 1997
Materials: Acrylic, steel, electronics
First shown at Snowcrash exhibition, Milan, 1997

TRAMP [80-81]
Easy Chair
Design: Timo Salli, 1996
Materials: Black and silver steel frame
First shown at Snowcrash exhibition, Milan, 1997
Later produced by Cappellini

ZIKZAK [60]
Collapsible chair
Design: Timo Salli, 1997
Materials: Steel, acrylic and stainless steel net
Dimensions: H80xW40xD50 cm
First shown at Snowcrash exhibition, Milan, 1997

GLOBLOW [173]
Design: Vesa Hinkola, Markus Nevalainen,
Rane Vaskivuori, 1996
Materials: Steel frame, rip-stop nylon, inflates
when switched on, 12 W fan inside
Dimensions: standard lamp 01, size fully inflated:
H1850xW800 mm
floor lamp 02, size fully inflated: H1600xW650 mm
hanging lamp, size fully inflated: W800 mm
wall lamp, size fully inflated: W650 mm
First shown at Helsinki Design Museum, 1996
Part of the Snowcrash Exhibition 1997
After 2003 produced by David Design
Later produced by David Design

DIGITAL FRESCO [45]
Animation
Design: Timo Vierros, 1997
Digitally restored by Marko Tandefelt, 2021
First shown at the Snowcrash exhibition, Milan, 1997

THE SNOWCRASH SOUNDTRACK [44]
Composer: Mika Vainio, aka Ø
Recorded at: Sähkö Recordings
First presented at the Snowcrash exhibition, Milan,
1997

DRESS CHAIR [90]
Design: Rane Vaskivuori, Timo Vierros, 1997
Materials: Steel frame, with powder coated finish,
100% nylon upholstery cover and polyether filling
Dimensions: H82xW75xD63 cm
First shown in the Marimekko fair stand at
Düsseldorf fair 199

KROMOSOM CHAIR [94]
Design: Jan Tromp, 1998
Materials: Form-pressed plywood, steel
Dimensions: H78xW48xD48 cm
First shown at Salone del Mobile, Milan, 1998 for
Artek

KROMOSOM TABLE
Design: Jan Tromp, 1998
Materials: Aluminium-faced plywood, steel
Dimensions: H73xW70xD70 cm
First shown at Stockholm Furniture Fair, 1999 for
Artek

ROLL LIGHT [101]
Floor lamp
Design: Ilkka Suppanen, 1998
Materials: Aluminium, composite textile of polymer
fibres
Dimensions: H145xW25xD25 cm
First shown at Stockholm Furniture Fair 1999

LESS IS MORE [100]
Space divider
Design: Simo Muir, 1998
Materials: Steel, Dacron fabric
Dimensions: H140xW160xD40 cm
First shown at Stockholm Furniture Fair 1999

DESK TOP [95]
Computer table
Design: Teppo Asikainen, Ilkka Terho, 1999
Materials: Glass, steel, polystyrene
Dimensions: H72xW180xD80 cm
First shown at Stockholm Furniture Fair 1999

TIMOTIMO LAMP [99]
Design: Timo Salli, 1998
Materials: Transparent and metallised polyester
Dimensions: H40xW40x5 cm
First shown at Stockholm Furniture Fair 1999

LAMPLAMP [96]
Design: Timo Salli, 1999
Materials: Transparent and metallised polyester
Dimensions: 40x40x5 cm
First shown at Stockholm Furniture Fair, 1999

FIREBOX [89]
Portable fireplace
Design:Timo Salli, 1999
First shown at Stockholm Furniture Fair, 1999

FLY CHAIR [92]
Design: Teppo Asikainen, 1999
Materials: Steel, stainless steel, synthetic fabric
Dimensions: H80xW45xD50 cm
First shown at Salone del Mobile, Milan, 1999

HI WAVE [106-107]
Pendant lamp
Design: Ilkka Suppanen, 1998
Materials: Polyester fabric, aluminium ceiling
fitting, aluminium light fitting
Dimensions: H100-160xW140xD147 / H100-
160xW270xD147cm / H100-160xW400xD147 cm (single,
double, triple in 2001)
First shown at Stockholm Furniture Fair, 1999

GAME SHELF [102-103]
Console table
Design: Ilkka Suppanen, 1999
Materials: Aluminium
Dimensions: H345xW1475xD350 cm
First shown at Salone del Mobile, Milan, 1999

SOUNDWAVE ACOUSTIC SERIES; SWELL [130]
Acoustic panel
Design: Teppo Asikainen, 1999
Materials: Moulded polyester fibre
Dimensions: H58,5xW58,5xD8 cm
Designed for restaurant Pravda, Helsinki, 1999
First shown at IFF Köln, 2000
After 2003 produced by Offecct
Later produced by Offecct

SLIP [142]
Space divider
Design: Rane Vaskivuori, Timo Vierros, 2001
Materials: Anodised aluminium profile, anodised aluminium/POM foot and polyester textile POM hook
Dimensions: H180/130/60xW118xD4 cm

INFINITE LIGHT [116-117]
VHS
Design: Arik Levy, 1999
Time: 60 minutes
Materials: VHS video tape in box case
First shown at Salone del Mobile, Milan, 2000

THING [118]
Hanging Lamp
Design: Arik Levy, 1999
Dimensions: 1-4,2 m
Materials: Telescope stick, carbon fibre
First shown at Salone del Mobile, Milan, 2000

BROADWAY
Table
Design: Teppo Asikainen, Ilkka Terho, 2000
First shown at Salone del Mobile, Milan, 2000

GLOBLOW LED [121]
Pendant Lamp
Design: Vesa Hinkola, Markus Nevalainen, Rane Vaskivuori, 2000
Materials: White rip-stop nylon
Dimensions: 75x75 cm
First shown at Salone del Mobile, Milan, 2000

LIGHT PUNCH [175]
Pendant lamp
Design: Markus Nevalainen, 2000
Materials: Transparent Xorel textile
Dimensions: H90xW30 cm
First shown at 100-Exhibition, Helsinki, 2000

FELTBOX [148]
Storage units
Design: Markus Nevalainen, Kari Sivonen, 2000
Materials: Moulded polyester fibre
Dimensions: 80x40x60 cm
First shown at Workspheres exhibition, MoMa, 2001
After 2003 produced by Softbox
Later produced by Softbox

LIFT ORGANISE-SYSTEM [149]
Design: Markus Nevalainen, Kari Sivonen, 2000
Materials: Stainless Steel
First shown at Workspheres exhibition, MoMa, 2001

LIFT STORAGE-SYSTEM
Design: Markus Nevalainen, Kari Sivonen, 2000
Materials: Stainless Steel
Dimensions: 172,7x184,8x42,5 cm
First shown at Workspheres exhibition, MoMa, 2001

GETSET [164-165]
Work desk
Design: Arik Levy, 2001
Materials: MDF, fibreglass-reinforced polyester, aluminium
Dimensions: Various sizes
First shown at Workspheres exhibition, MoMa, 2001

ADDAPT [146]
Clip-on bags
Design: Arik Levy, 2001
Materials: Polyester fabric, aluminium hooks
Dimensions: Gym Bag H34xW37xD23 cm; Office bag H32xW37xD10 cm; Computer bag H32xW37xD7 cm; Wallet Pocket H27xW37xD0,5 cm; Travel bag – Unfolded H70xW37xD10 cm Folded H35xW37xD10 cm
First shown at Workspheres exhibition, MoMa, 2001

LOCO [143]
Portable work pad
Design: Ilkka Suppanen, 2001
Materials: Polyester fabric
Dimensions: Open H71xW107 cm Folded H40xW37xD8 cm.
First shown at Workspheres exhibition, MoMa, 2001

SOUNDWAVE ACOUSTIC SERIES; SCRUNCH [130]
Acoustic panel
Design: Teppo Asikainen, 2001
Materials: Moulded polyester fibre
Dimensions: H58,5xW58,5xD8,0 cm

First shown at Stockholm Furniture Fair, 2001
After 2003 produced by Offecct
Later produced by Offecct

SOUNDWAVE ACOUSTIC SERIES; SWOOP [131]
Acoustic panel
Design: Teppo Asikainen, 2002
Materials: Moulded polyester fibre
Dimensions: H58,5xW58,5xD8,0 cm
After 2003 produced by Offecct
Later produced by Offecct

SOUNDWAVE ACOUSTIC SERIES; SWELL DIFFUSER
Acoustic diffuser panel
Design: Teppo Asikainen, 2002
Materials: PET
Dimensions: H58,5xW58,5xD8,0 cm
First Shown at Stockholm Furniture Fair 2001
After 2003 produced by Offecct
Later produced by Offecct

GLOBLOW POLE [179]
Pendant lamp
Design: Vesa Hinkola, Markus Nevalainen, Rane Vaskivuori, 2002
Materials: White rip-stop nylon
Dimensions: 126x50 cm

CLOUD [158-159]
Inflatable, mobile room
Design: Monica Förster, 2002
Materials: White rip-stop nylon, fan and bag included
Dimensions: H230xW400xD530 cm
First shown at Salone del Mobile, 2000
After 2003 produced by Offecct
Later produced by Offecct

THE SOUND SOLUTION COLLECTION; PEACE ZONE, COOL & CALM, SAFE SILENCE, IN-BE-TWEEN, STILL WATER, WIDE TIDE [123-127]
Acoustic textiles
Design: Ulrika Mårtensson, 2000-2003
Materials: Wool, paper cord and viscose
Dimensions: 145 (or 70) x 280 cm
After 2003 produced by Ludvig Svensson
Later produced by Ludvig Svensson

TAKSI CHAIR [167]
Design: Jan Tromp, 2002
Materials: Wood beads, climbing cords and extruded aluminium frame
Dimensions: H90xW60xD60 cm

Jane Withers is a British curator, design consultant and writer. Since 2001 she runs Jane Withers Studio in London, known for conducting projects that address environmental issues through the lens of design—working with institutions and brands internationally such as Kvadrat (DK), V&A Museum (UK) and Design Museum (UK).

Ilkka Suppanen is a Finnish designer based in Helsinki and Milan. He established Studio Suppanen in 1995 and is one of the founding members of Snowcrash. His interdisciplinary office moves between architecture, furniture and product design as well as art commissions for clients such as Cappellini (IT), Panasonic (JP) and Iittala (FI).

Gustaf Kjellin is a Swedish curator based in Stockholm. He is the curator of the exhibition *Snowcrash* at Nationalmuseum in Stockholm (2021), editor of the publication *Design & Peace* for the Alvar Aalto Foundation (2019) and co-author of the book *Helt vildt! — The Second Golden Age of Danish Design* (2018).

This book is made with generous support from

The Robert Weil Family Foundation
Proventus
Arkkitehtuuritoimisto Valvomo OY
Studio Suppanen
Nationalmuseum
Kulturfonden för Sverige och Finland

Thank you to everyone who has shared their stories, and to all those connected to or employed at Snowcrash who are not mentioned in the book but contributed from beginning to end!

Writers: Jane Withers, Gustaf Kjellin
Editor: Ilkka Suppanen
Graphic design: Fredrik Bohman, Gustaf Kjellin
Copy editor: Hannah Clarkson
Publisher: Marie Arvinius
Repro: JK Morris Production
Print and binding: Livonia Print SIA, 2021 Latvia

ISBN 978-91-89270-10-7

Published in 2021 by
Arvinius + Orfeus Publishing AB
Olivecronas väg 4, 113 61 Stockholm, Sweden
Phone +46 8 32 00 15
info@ao-publishing.com
www.ao-publishing.com

© 2021 Arvinius + Orfeus Publishing
All Rights Reserved

This book is protected by copyright law and international treaties. All rights are reserved by the copyright owners. No part of the book may be reproduced in any form by any electronic or mechanical means (including photocopying, recording or information storage and retrieval) without the prior written permission of Arvinius + Orfeus Publishing AB.

Image and photograph credits

Courtesy of Arkkitehtuuritoimisto Valvomo OY: 6–7, 12, 15–21, 26–27, 50–55, 91–93, 108–109, 149
Courtesy of The Estate of R. Buckminster Fuller: 10
© Tuomas Marttila: 28–29, 57, 70–71, 94–95, 167–168
© Marco Melander: 31, 60–61, 99–101
Courtesy of Timo Salli: 32–33, 88–89, 96–97
© Jens Andersson: 35–39, 62–69, 72–73, 79–83, 90, 102–107, 116–117, 121, 123–127, 130–131, 144–145, 148, 150–151, 160–161, 171–173, 175–181
Courtesy of Ilkka Suppanen: 40–41, 44, 49
Courtesy of Marko Tandefelt Parasense Helsinki: 45
© PH: M Pignata Monti: 47
© P Wahlgren: 58–58
© Ninna Kuismanen: 74–74
© Moviestore Collection Ltd / Alamy Stock Photo: 85
Courtesy of Andreas Murray: 87, 128, 163
Courtesy of Mikko Karvonen, Mika Ilari Koskinen, Niko Punin: 113
Courtesy of Lars Fuhre: 113
© Alexander Crispin: 118, 142, 143, 146–147, 164–165
Courtesy of Vesa Hinkola: 120
© Tham & Videgård: 133
© Åke E:son Lindman: 134–141
Courtesy of Hans Anderson and Johan Svensson: 152–153, 155, 157
© Anna Danielsson / Nationalmuseum: 158–159
© Bukowskis: 183
© Kanayama Akira and Tanaka Atsuko Association. Courtesy of Nakanoshima Museum of Art, Osaka: 184
© Chao Han via https://www.cluvens.net: 185
© Herman Miller: 187 (top)
© Sundahl, Sune / ArkDes: 187 (bottom)
© Verner Panton Design AG. Design by Verner Panton @vernerpantonofficial: 188
© mmw.no / Jiri Havran: 189
© Mitsuru Mizutani. Courtesy of Kosuke Tsumura: 190
© Instituto Bardi / Casa de Vidro: 191
© Noam Preisman. Courtesy of Magasin III, Jaffa: 194
© Holmén, Erik / Nordiska museet: 195
© Swedese: 196